Manifesting Miracles

A collection of manifesting success stories from around the world

Book 1 of the Manifesting Success Stories Series

Zehra Mahoon & Friends

Do you have a compelling manifestation success story of your own?

Submit your story for publication in the next volume of the
Manifesting Success Book Series

To find out more about submission guidelines visit www.zmahoon.com

Dedication
To All Boundless Spirits

Royalties from this work are being directed to
The Boundless School
Ontario, Canada

Registered Canadian Charity #124225855RR0001

Imagine learning environmental science by creating, tending and harvesting your own organic garden. How about reciting poetry for English class by going on blindfolded night hikes in thunderstorms to find your muse. How about learning math by designing a business plan to manage a successful conservation area. If you plan to create more trails, go out and make them yourselves.

When you come home from a long day, you live, dine and clean side by side with your peers and teachers. And when you lose your shit, you have a caring mental health team to help you find your equilibrium.
Steven Gottlieb
Founder, Executive Director

Stories are in alphabetical order based on first names

Contents

Acknowledgments

My heartfelt thanks to all the authors who helped to make this book possible. A special thank you to Kinza Mahoon for cover design and Nicole Hale for coordination and editorial support.

Zehra

Do you have a compelling manifestation success story of your own?

Submit your story for publication in the next volume of the
Manifesting Success Book Series

To find out more about submission guidelines visit www.zmahoon.com

Why this book?

I have compiled this book for three reasons.

First, I often get asked to share stories about manifesting success. I think that stories, especially from real people who have real life struggles similar to our own provide us with hope that life can improve. And hope is perhaps the most important of all human emotions, for even love cannot exist where there is no hope.

Secondly, I find that stories can be used to demonstrate how to use the Law of Attraction when we not only share the outward manifestation, but also the inward self-talk, thoughts and emotions. In this manner they are a powerful learning tool.

Lastly, who doesn't like good story? Stories are more memorable than theory. Reading stories of manifesting success is a wonderful way to pass a lazy afternoon while learning something valuable and energizing ourselves with the emotion of hope.

It is my intention to bring you a wide range of situations that will help you to see how the Law of Attraction plays out, so that you will be able to utilize this knowledge to your advantage.

What is a miracle?

I don't know what your definition of a miracle is, but by my definition when something happens that you did not think was possible, it is termed to be a miracle.

When you start understanding the Law of Attraction, you are able to see the miracle in every day little things. When you ask for something and the Universe delivers, not just what you asked for but more – that is a miracle.

Most people think that a miracle is something big, but to me, miracles come in all sorts of shapes and sizes, for I know that it does not take the Universe any more effort or energy to create a parking space compared to winning a jackpot. So I call my parking spaces "Million Dollar" parking spaces – they are miracles that remind me that the Universe is listening and responding to even my smallest and most unimportant desires.

This book is about appreciating both big and small miracles for the more we appreciate the more we bring things that reflect our appreciation into our lives.

Be Realistic...
EXPECT MIRACLES
Dr. Wayne Dyer

What is the Law of Attraction

"Law of Attraction" is a new label for age old wisdom. It is basically all about keeping a positive outlook and looking at all life situations from a place of hope.

Law of Attraction incorporates strategies to deal with negative beliefs, worry and anxiety and different life situations based on identifying the vibrational essence of emotions. The underlying premise is "like attracts like" meaning that to attract positive outcomes we need to think positive thoughts.

One of the most fundamental aspects of the Law of Attraction is that it promotes trust and faith in the Universe; helping us to see that we are connected to the Universe and that our intuition is guidance from the Universe.

Law of Attraction, and more specifically the teachings of Abraham-Hicks help us to understand how to interpret the emotional component of our thoughts, since a thought is positive or negative based on this emotional component.

Lastly, when you really go deep into it, Law of Attraction provides a way for us to bridge religion and spirituality with science and quantum physics.

For a better understanding of the Law of Attraction please refer to the Law of Attraction by Esther & Jerry Hicks and Thrive by Zehra Mahoon.

How to have a good day, every day

By Adelyn Robinett

Hi, my name is Addy and I am inspired to be a Unicorn!

My story started four and a half years ago when I arrived six weeks early, eager to start my mission on Earth. The Universe took care of everything I needed and I knew I would be okay.

I want to tell you why being a Unicorn is important to me. I have always been aware that everything around me is beautiful and has a place on this planet, just like me. I have been learning from my mom and my grandma that the more I appreciate the more I see everything with that much more love. I start my every morning saying "Good Morning Mom, Sun's up, what kind of special thing are we going to do today?" She always says "I don't know Addy, what do you want to do today?" I say, I want to do something magical and fun! And my day is always fun!

My grandma tells me that my smile brightens her day. So, you know, if it works on her, I know it will work on anyone I meet. Smiling brings joy and sometimes it turns into laughter. I like things that make me happy. It makes me happy to think that all that is asleep in winter will wake up in the spring and brand new flowers will smell good to the bees making their honey. I love honey!

I also have my night friends who come out just before dark. Some make noise and some light the night, which tells me soon I will see stars if the sky is clear. I love looking at the stars and singing to them – you know "twinkle, twinkle little stars" I love that rhyme.

So, you see, I haven't seen much yet but I am learning that the more I am aware of my happy thoughts the more fun I have. There is so much that makes me happy and brings me joy and I could keep going but I always remember to tell the ones who are close and who are in my life, I love them and that I know there is a lot to be happy about. I will keep on bringing joy into my day by saying "the sun's up, what kind of special thing am I going to do today?" and then make that happen by a smile and a happy thought.

To all Unicorns: we are special.

A Note from the Universe:
Keep believing in the magic of the Unicorns. All things are possible, when you believe. Love everyone around you and spread your magic where ever you go. Always be guided by your heart. Everyone is learning. Even your grandmother is learning. Don't think that because she is older that she knows more than you. The best thing that she can teach you is to not care much about what others think- you be you. Follow your heart and trust that the Universe is guiding you and watching over you all the time. Trust your feelings. When you feel good you are heading the right way. When you feel bad, it means that you are looking at things in a way that the Universe wants you to change.

A strong desire will always override any obstacles

By Andrea Roman

I remember telling my friends "I feel so bad inside all of the time and I don't know why. I don't want to but I do". I was just a teenager at the time, but my life felt unbearable. I used to think "how is this even possible? I am a good person. I never harm anybody so why are these things happening to me?". I even felt that the life I was living is not my life at all like I was living someone else's life. Most days I would be engrossed in my thoughts about my life, trying to figure out why things were the way they were; trying to figure out a way to fix it all.

During those dark gloomy days, the one thing that lit up my day was listening to Michael Jackson. I was a huge fan. It was my biggest desire to see him in person. The appreciation I felt for him distracted me from the everyday difficult reality I was experiencing. I remember I was so stuck in negative and worrisome thoughts, I wanted to change them, but I didn't know how. Over the years, I have learned that, it didn't feel like my own life, because I was not in alignment with my own Inner Being, because I was looking at things in a way that made me unhappy – it was my perspective.

My desire for change brought me to the discovery of a new hobby of creating a group of pen pals with Michael Jackson fans and building a community. We shared our love for collecting magazines and DVDs which was a lot of fun for me because finally I felt at home; I felt understood and I fit into this new community, and my life started changing. I understand now that the distraction that the new hobby afforded me put me in a state of appreciation and love for the most part of my day. I started feeling better, I was spending most of my time talking with like-minded people. My life started feeling better as a result. Then one day I heard the news that Michael Jackson was coming to my country! I couldn't believe it! I made up my mind that I must go to see him perform.

It was not going to be easy. First, there was the question of being able to buy the ticket – I had to come up with the money. Then there was the question of traveling to the other end of the country on my own for the very first time – of course, my parents were not happy about this, and to be honest it felt a little scary. Until then I hadn't really travelled very far from home, just a few short trips with my friends once in a while.

It was unbelievable how things came together so smoothly.

Despite all of my worries my mother never said I shouldn't go and she even paid for my ticket and the train ticket too. A big feeling of relief came over me as a part of my worries were gone. The second part got even easier as I met a group of fans on the train who were also headed to the concert and we all decided to stick together all the way through our trip. Everything happened so fast. All the months of waiting in eager anticipation of this magical moment which was over in a couple of hours. I think I must have been in the Vortex big time because I've never felt so good before. Since then, I learned to access my Vortex deliberately using meditation on a daily basis.

Looking back at it now, I understand an important Law of Attraction principle: "A strong desire will always override any obstacle", as long as you avoid focusing on and thinking about all the obstacles on your path to it.

This is my ticket to the Michael Jackson concert.

My journey with the Law of Attraction

Ever since I was a teenager, I knew there's a deeper connection between what I wanted and what I got. Two important things caught my attention and these things represent the basic elements of my present belief system which I have built upon over the years.

My first observation was that every time I turn my focus upon something, smaller signs would show up that correlated with my object of focus. The more attention I gave to that topic or object the more things would show up until eventually, it would turn out the way I it wanted to.

The second was: my belief that any desire comes true, sooner or later but it eventually comes true. At that time, I did not know that the buffer of time between asking and getting it is in my hands.

What I was about to learn years later by listening to numerous teachers was that feeling good is the name of the game and yes I can feel good regardless of what is going on around me. This state is called "being in the Vortex" by collective teachers called Abraham channeled by Esther Hicks. I have so much appreciation for them and even up to this date I find their teachings to be the leading edge on the subject of the Law of Attraction. Listening to their numerous audio workshops I have learned how to be deliberate in my life and how to control the way I feel and therefore my point attention. However, at the beginning, I wasn't up to speed with their teachings and I have found it a bit difficult to understand their concepts and explanations and started listening to other teachers like Louise Hay, Wayne Dyer, Iyanla Vanzant (whom I've found really funny and I could really relate to what she was saying at her workshops). After a while, I returned to Abraham and everything clicked into place this time.

Manifesting a happy, balanced life in a deliberate way

Manifesting a happy, balanced life in a deliberate way is like building a house only it's never getting done because you are always renovating it. The most important component in the building process is consistency. There is a bit of work involved with being happy, which I know sounds a bit weird because being happy should really be easy. Yeah right, it's easy when you observe something good. Try to be happy when everything around you is falling apart ... it's not easy at all.

And here comes the "secret": you can be happy if you choose to – because happiness is a decision. It sounds easy but it takes quite a bit of practice to achieve it. Over the years I have discovered what works best for me and it is, in fact, two things combined: Meditation, first thing in the morning, and the second appreciating everything that I can, even the smallest things in my life. These two things combined make the difference. When I do this, I am able to transform reality into whatever I want. I am not kidding you.

I also have a confession to make, sometimes when things are going well I get lazy about doing the two things that are my secret recipe, simply enjoying how good things are. But soon enough I notice something negative and then something unwanted hits me and I go "Where did that come from?" and I can tell what went wrong if I look back and pay attention. However, as soon as I start realigning everything works out like magic.

Links to my YouTube channel and website:
https://www.youtube.com/c/LawofAttractionTheEssence/featured
https://lawofattractiontheessence.com/

A note from the Universe:
Indeed, when you ask for something it is always given, and nothing is ever held back – you must allow it to manifest. Every desire is heard and responded to even if it never comes to your lips. Solutions to every problem and every obstacle on your path are created and ready for execution. Your excitement is the key to it all. Remain excited about your life and the Universe will move mountains to surprise and delight you. Excitement comes from birthing new desires. When you let the excitement of what you are reaching for call you forward, the obstacles disappear from your path. Always keep your eye on the prize and trust that everything you need will show up for you. *Success is certain when the desire is bigger than the fear.* Your desire to see Michael Jackson was so big that the fear of travelling alone and not having the money was puny in comparison – and so nothing could get in your way. Make your desires exciting and your fears puny, for the Universe does not put any obstacles on your path, you put them there with your fear. When you think thoughts that make the fear inconsequential to the achievement of your desire, then it must be.

Wishes do come true! I manifested a trip to Disney World with my children, all paid.

By Brandi Parks

I used all the tools I had heard about with deliberate intention, and the results were better than anything I had ever imagined. I had heard that you have to believe that anything is possible, but I wasn't sure that just believing would be enough? But I said to myself "no harm in giving it a shot? We won't be any worse off for trying".

This is how it happened.

I really wanted my children to see Mickey Mouse and all that Disney World has to offer and I wanted to do it while they were still in that age group where the magic of Disney means so much. I had never been anywhere like that before and I was determined to get us all there.

I had been learning about the Law of Attraction and I thought to myself, why not use it to try and take my two children to Disney that year. I didn't know how it would happen because in reality, I did not have enough money as a single Mom to make it happen It was seemingly impossible. I didn't know how but I knew I had to believe it in order for it to happen.

I didn't know if just believing it would be enough so I had to get to work in feeling that the impossible was about to happen. I had heard that the universe has an endless supply of abundance if we could just tap into it. I truly did believe in the power of the Universe to bring us everything we desire.

I let my mind experience the joy of us being at Disney. I looked at flights, hotel rentals and tickets. I put the dates in my calendar and planned to take off from work. I wrote our itinerary. I imagined us running to hug Mickey in excitement. I imagined the fun we would have on the rides. I watched videos of Splash Mountain and could see us drenched with water at the end of the ride. I visualized my daughter dancing with all the Disney Princesses. I saw my son playing with Alvin and the Chipmunks. Somehow it would happen. I did my part in creating the space and visualized the joy on my children's faces.

I called a friend and told her about our upcoming trip like it was already planned and paid for. I posted on social media asking for tips on a trip to Disney. In other words, everything about it felt real. We were going to Disney.

The following morning my boyfriend asked if I had talked to his mother. "No", I said "does she want me to call her?" He had this look on his face as if he was trying to hide a very big secret but just couldn't keep it in. Then he spilled the beans! He said his Mom called him that morning and invited us all to go to Disney World and she was buying the tickets and covered every expense, even food and travel! It was better than anything I had planned in my head. We had reservations at the Magic Kingdom Resort along with an extra few days vacation at the beach! It was even more amazing than I expected it to be and we had the time of our lives!

What I learned from that experience is that anything truly is possible when you believe that it is and when you allow the Universe to figure out all the details. I think that the magic ingredient was the fact that I wanted it but I wasn't worrying about it – instead I was excited. I wasn't wondering how I would "make it happen" and yet I was believing that it would. I learned that trying to make things happen is much harder than letting the Universe take over.

Connect with Brandi on Facebook
www.facebook.com/groups/537823830244476/

A note from the Universe:
You asked and your desire was big so it had to be. The fact that you were not afraid is what sealed the deal. You were not afraid to ask. And you were not afraid to enjoy the process of asking. Most people are afraid of asking, because they are afraid of being disappointed. The funny thing about it is that *the fear of disappointment is what leads to disappointment*.

You were willing to tell your friends about your desire, and in doing so you declared to all who could hear your confidence in a positive unfolding. And so it could be no other way. Where there is doubt, then the powerful Law of Attraction will make that doubt a reality.

Most people are so afraid of what others will say if things don't work out that they become fearful of asking, or worse, they ask and then they start thinking of all the reasons why their desires cannot come to fruition. If only all humans could be bold enough to ask and stand in the absolute knowing that they can have, be or do anything they want, then there would be no misery on planet Earth for all humans would be asking and manifesting all their heart's desires. Remember: *You can control the outcome, if you stop trying to control the path.* You wanted it, you stayed focused on it, but you did not try to control "how" it would come about and so it did. Go about all your goals in this way and you will create a magical life.

A pandemic blessing

By Camilla Searcy

This story started last year as my girlfriends and I were celebrating my birthday, they asked me what I would like to come my way this year to mark a millstone in life. Before I knew it, I was saying I needed more me-time and more girlfriend time! The very next day we were hit with the 2020 pandemic which spiraled into everybody being in lockdown at home for many days. I had manifested the me-time I wanted! I tried to find my way to be unconditional and just slow down and take the time to get to know me! Wasn't sure how long we would be off so I took advantage of meditating every day and finding joy in everything. It is not everyday you get to stay home, get paid, and get the time to focus on yourself.

One day, my husband Pat, and I decided to do some yard work. We have so many different species of daffodils that were planted before we moved to the house we lived in. Every year they keep multiplying so that now we have a garden full of them looking rather unkempt. I told my husband, "I wish I could give some of these flowers or bulbs away". He agreed "yeah, we have plenty of them to give away, but whose going to take them? We should just get rid of them and clean up the garden". Guess what? It wasn't even one minute later that a truck pulls up and stops on the side of the road and a man gets out and comes over there to where my husband and I are working. "I know it's the pandemic and everything but my little girl rides the bus by here and she says she sees the hillside with all these beautiful flowers so I was wondering if we could stop and pick some?" he said.

How amazing, I thought! "Oh my gosh yes! Of course! Do you need a bucket or a bag and a shovel?" I said, really excited that now my flowers will not go to waste. "No, I've got something in my truck that will work" he said, and walked back to the truck. He returns with his daughter, she was probably around eight and looked so excited. She came up to Pat and I and introduced her self then she said to her dad "Oh my goodness dad there's so many flowers, I want them all". The father said "honey just pick a few".

The father told me that she just lost her grandfather just that week and they were not able to go to the funeral because of the pandemic. Her grandfather used to have daffodils just like ours in his yard so she really wanted some of our flowers. He was so grateful that we let him and his daughter pick as many flowers as they wanted. I just sat there and enjoyed watching them share a special time as they dug up the flowers. It was so enlightening to see something that I just said happen almost instantaneously right in front of my eyes. I keep telling my husband "see Pat, see it does really happen". He sees it happen all the time with me but he doesn't understand how any of it works and doesn't believe that I'm making it happen, nevertheless he is amazed when it does!

So as the days went on I thought I would see if my girlfriend would have time to make some jewelry for me. I gave her a call and she agreed! I was thrilled! Within the months to follow, I had my sister-in-law, my nieces, and my cousins all getting together for graduations. And there it was, I was getting what I wanted, more girlfriend time! These opportunities kept happening and it was exciting! I was manifesting what I wanted.

I didn't know that my next manifestation was already starting to play out. My friend who had made my jewelry told me about this group that that she is involved in. She was learning things that she thought I would be interested in. She invited me to join the The 40 Day Law of Attraction Challenge! So began the next chapter of my life! Yep, there it was, things were turning out better then I imagined, and the group that was doing the challenge was so kind and caring, I was hooked! I started learning a lot more about myself. I discovered why, in the past, I would have these synchronistic things happen to me. Since I've been in this group I have learned more about why life unfolds the way it does and yes! it's true, I've got more girlfriends. (YAY ME!) Like one of my new girlfriends, Nancy, would say (GO ME!).

The funny thing was, months before I had been searching on the internet for a special fragrance with my favorite sandalwood scent and found a perfume called Zahra so I ordered it. Wow, there it was! Soon after It arrived, I met a new friend and her name Zehra! The synchronicities are mind blowing! What are the chances? Since then, I have learned that these synchronicities are the way in which the Universe communicates with us.

Recently I met a lady at a place that I frequent. She had moved here from Connecticut and only has one family member living in our town. She and I were waiting at the pharmacy, and we started talking. Before I knew it, we became friends and have been hanging out, going places and getting to know each other. I found out that she too is into the same things that I am into! Proving the principle "like attracts like". To this day I look back at that moment, when I had asked for more girlfriend time and smile with joy and an inner knowing that I was in control, creating all of it! I even told one of the girls I had that dinner with that I have had more girlfriend time in the last year than when I was growing up! We just laughed she said, well that is what you wished for!

I have my own proof now that when you have a desire, and it is strong enough and you believe that it is possible, you will get results! I continue to believe that you can have, be and do anything you desire. I continue on the journey of being mindful and appreciate all I have and I am grateful for the beauty around me. I hope that my sharing my story will inspire you into knowing that you too can get what you desire. Be true to yourself and your beliefs, and you will soon notice that manifesting what you want is easy and fun. I hope you have enjoyed my story as much as I have enjoyed sharing it! Remember You are the Center of your own Universe and you can create ANYTHING and it will be Beautiful!

A note from the Universe:
The Universe has a full view of everyone and everything and it is easy for the Law of Attraction to match the desire of one with the desire of another. This is co-creation at it's best.

When a desire is pure and not tainted with doubt or fear, it flows easily into manifestation. It is difficult for humans to understand how easy it is for the Universe to choreograph the dance of creation to perfection, but you only have to look around you to understand. Who among humans can make the sun rise? Who among humans can make the seasons come and go? Is it therefore too big a stretch to lend your trust to the Universe in the knowing that you are loved and adored. You are guided and you are provided for, for you are an extension of that which is the Source of all things. Remember: *that it is as easy to create a castle as a button*. Big desires and small desires are all the same to the Universe; one is not bigger or less important or less urgent than the other. It is your belief that one is small and the other big, and that one will take more time that the other or more effort or more resources than the other that creates the difference. *From the vantage point of the Universe all desires are equal.*

I manifested John by using the Law of Attraction

By Cindy Knowler

After many years of an abusive marriage and inappropriate partners I realized I was attracting the wrong people and unhappiness in my relationships. I reached a point where I didn't want to create more of the same. As I thought about my life, I decided I needed to take time for me, to love and appreciate myself and others, to enjoy my own company, and I did exactly that. I didn't realize I was creating and manifesting through using what I now know is the Law of Attraction. Now I know that there is power in giving up. When I gave up trying to control the outcomes in my life, everything started working out for me. Most of all I started feeling peaceful and looking forward to living instead of being afraid of what else might go wrong.

My wish was to feel financially secure by having my mortgage paid off as soon as possible. I didn't know how. Then one day, out of the blue one of my colleagues started telling me about how excited she was that her financial advisor had shown her a way to pay off her mortgage faster. I asked her to introduce me to her, and I was surprised by how easy she made it seem to have my mortgage paid off many years sooner than I thought I would. Looking back on it now I can see how the Law of Attraction orchestrated that for me. I also understand that it happened easily because I didn't worry about it. It was a wish, I put it out there and forgot about it and then everything fell into place effortlessly.

My next desire was to be able to retire early, downsize to put a nest egg away and be able to travel while I was still young. Out of the blue, my company offered me an early retirement package at age 48 and I appreciated that I was able to take it, because I had already laid the foundation for it. For the next year I travelled to wonderful places. I had more time and fun with my family and wonderful friends. I volunteered with VON (Victorian Order of Nurses) helping seniors in their homes. I did things I loved.

Next, I decided I wanted a part time job to supplement my income, and took the first job I was offered. I was satisfied with that job but found another job that was better, and another job that was even better and financially perfect for me with perfect hours that matched my preference. All of this was happening "because" I wasn't trying. Yes, that's right, I now know that if you're trying hard to "make" something happen, it takes longer because trying puts blockages on your path. You see, trying implies manipulation; we don't need to manipulate things to knock them into place. We can just let them be and let the Universe sort them out.

I paid off my mortgage just a month before I was let go from that job during the 2008 recession. Perfect timing, orchestrated by the Law of Attraction once more!

I was happy, and positive and I had self-worth for the first time in my life since childhood. I wanted more. This time my wish was to downsize and move near water and trees, something I have always wanted to do. I found the perfect house at the perfect price and made new friends.

A group of us would get together regularly at the local community center and hang out. We had so much fun and did everything as a group.

One day I wrote down the qualities I would like in a partner; forgot about it, and carried on just having fun. About a year later, our group had planned to meet for an activity at the community center, but for one reason or another no one showed up except me and John. I knew John because he participated in our group, but never really got to know him or talk to him. That evening we decided we would go ahead with our plans for the evening without the others. We had such a good time, so many laughs, and I was so glad we didn't cancel altogether. A couple of weeks later he asked me on a date...and the rest, as they say is history. I manifested this wonderful man through the Law of Attraction, by thinking about what I wanted and letting it go. He is everything on my list and more.

A note from the Universe:
When you stop controlling the outcome and find a way to be satisfied with your life, you move forward on a smooth path. Satisfaction in the now moment does not mean that you no longer have goals or desires, or that you are not moving forward towards them. It merely means that you are not throwing tantrums along the way.

At any juncture in your life journey you can make the decision to be happy and satisfied; you can begin to start appreciating what you do have as opposed to complaining about what you don't have, and what you want will flow easily into your life. Remember: *there is no way to happiness; happiness is the way.* When you become fixated on a desire and start wondering when it will happen and how it will happen, you start drifting away from satisfaction, and this slows things down. Your desires would manifest easily if you would just let the Universe steer you, while you enjoy the ride.

Putting love first

By Claire & Richard Hirst

How Claire remembers it

In December 2019 one of our cats was run over, my autistic daughter and I were heartbroken. My partner of ten years lived nearby, I was afraid of him, his control and his narcissism. I had no money. Fibromyalgia and M.E. were making life impossible for me. I felt trapped.

I fostered kittens for a local charity, a guy was interested in adopting one. I liked Richard the second I heard his voice; he was soft spoken and I felt safe, comfortable and at peace around him when we met. He would message me to tell me how Lucy – the kitten was doing.

Hang on, I wasn't single! We stayed chatting strictly about cats. I knew my feelings were telling me something was changing. I had felt for many years that somewhere, there was another, better life for me. Feelings tell us everything don't they? My feelings were telling me that Richard HAD to be a part of my life.

How Richard remembers it

Richard had had a distressing divorce in 2012, followed by several years of severe anxiety and isolation. He had given up expecting anyone would be interested in him romantically, he just wanted to love a cat. Claire was already in a relationship. He'd decided Claire was:

1) Unavailable
2) Twelve years younger and this precluded him
3) Living too far away
4) Responsible for numerous pets

5) Unable to spend time away from her daughter

As a result of this kind of thinking from both sides the relationship was halted before it began; we could see no way forward. The perceived rock in the road seemed unsurmountable.

In March 2020 England went into Covid 19 lockdown. The thought of not being able to see each other was painful. It made us think again. Now I understood! This was it! My chance, my only chance. So, after some tears and a poor night's sleep, we had some manifesting to do. The next morning every one of these 'problems' were gone! Because our thinking changed literally overnight. Within 6 weeks we moved in together, a month later engaged. We married on 21st June 2021. It was and still is absolutely perfect.

Our poor thinking had kept us trapped. Our egos were telling us to listen to fearful thoughts to keep us safe; that to have what we wanted would be an intolerable risk. In fact, the real risk was to live without each other.

We now know how to differentiate between helpful warnings and unhelpful self-limiting beliefs; THE WAY YOU FEEL gives you either a red light or a green light. Having known about the power of intuition for many years, for us both it took faith and courage to dare to trust that intuition. Putting what we'd learned into practice brought instant results! We both reported the following qualities about the way in which our union manifested:

1) The 'rocks in the road' disappeared instantly

2) It was effortless
3) It felt generous, like we were receiving something wonderful
4) There was an astounding quality to it; there were no problems, even though nothing external had yet changed
5) It felt good, safe, comfortable and not risky
6) There were no doubts, just green lights all the way and an urgency to proceed
7) A sudden realisation that `being stuck' is usually no more than a psychological state constructed by your ego on the false premise of `keeping you safe'. Whenever you FEEL good about making any life changing decisions, there can be little or no danger at all

We're learning that the manifesting principles remain the same regardless of the subject matter. Richard had wondered "if it [manifesting] works for money, why doesn't it also work for relationships?" He now can tell you it does!

Financially, life slowly began to change in 2006 on holiday for Richard when he bought, for just one escudo, a used book about stock market investing. He started buying a few common stocks when he could.

Richard had failed mathematics miserably at school and knew nothing about business, finance or economics. But to him growing a portfolio was the easiest thing as the Universe knew he was ready. Now I'm doing the same and so is our daughter. Financially for now we have plateaued, though we have in life all we need.

We are appreciative and grateful. We have no interest in impressing anyone, we don't intend to manifest a Tesla car or a house that 'wows' onlookers. We are using the Law of Attraction to manifest feelings of peace, love, gratitude, serenity, health and wellbeing. Asking for peace of mind and love seems a reasonable request of the Universe.

You don't attract what you want, but rather what you are. If we align ourselves with the energy or attractor patterns of how we want things to feel, we must attract experiences to match. I've learned not to make big decisions when I feel low down on the emotional scale.

Though Richard's part-time receptionist job earned him a take-home-pay of just twelve thousand pounds per year, he was just able to afford to retire in 2020 at the age of fifty-one years. Now he could live for free, albeit modestly. His anxiety problems began to improve now he was no longer working for the mental health charity. Such a shift in environment allowed him time for self-care on a whole new level. He adopted a kitten called Lucy and met and married his soul-mate Claire.

We both laughed when we realised how difficult, even unnatural it felt to declare that we were "happy". We looked left and right to see if anyone was going to tell us off for saying such a thing. Old habits die hard.

If the Law of Attraction works for money and relationships, why doesn't it work for health? That's our next chapter. As we both want peace of mind and stress-free lives, we feel sure our physical health will improve in a more beautiful calm environment. Next we intend to manifest our perfect home further North within the Yorkshire Dales National Park.

A note from the Universe:
Everything works the same way for the law of the Universe are consistent and dependable. You can manifest all things the same way you manifest one thing.

Contrast is a powerful force. When you know what you don't want, you immediately know what you do want. You knew you could not let the pandemic keep you apart; therefore, you knew what you wanted. Once you know what you want, it is easy to brush aside all objections. Law of Attraction is a matching mechanism that works with precision every time. It will bring you more of whatever you give your attention to. It is important to understand that the Law of Attraction does not respond to your intention. It responds to your attention. Where before your intention was to love, your attention was on all the reasons why you should not permit love. When you had clarity that the most important thing was to be together all your objections melted away and your intention and attention become aligned. Whether it is a relationship you want or money, or a property or health, everything works the same way. Remember: *you ask, it is given and you must align your attention with your intention in order for it to be manifest.*

What did I do to attract this?

By Cristina Ishii

You know when something happens, and we wonder why it happened to us?

What did we do to attract it? I had been feeling down, discouraged and deflated for various reasons for more than a month. And then to add to it on top, my phone protective case broke in one corner and it stretched and got really lose causing my phone to slip and fall out. This was not the reason for my bad state of mind, but you know how it is, when you are feeling beat up every little thing makes it worse.

So now I was thinking, Oh No, I'll have to go online and order a new case; I don't even know what to order, and what if it won't fit my phone? I decided it might work better to check out a store.

I spotted a really small store which is just outside Loblaws (a grocery store chain in Canada), it was convenient and really, I wasn't looking for anything fancy, and I just happened to be there shopping for grocery. I asked the guy behind the counter if he could help me find a replacement case for my Samsung S9+ phone.

He says let me make a phone call and turns away. Meanwhile, I'm thinking "really? You have to make a phone call to find me a cover for my phone?" Then I heard him talking away about some cases he had in the back and I thought there is no storage at the back of the store, so it must just be a cupboard.

Browsing around as I waited for him to get off the phone, I saw an Otterbox case for my phone model on display. A couple of weeks prior when the thought of replacing my phone cover was not up for consideration, I had heard how wonderful the Otterbox products were, but I wasn't really picky. Then I thought, this is the Law of Attraction in action.

He finished his call and said, "this case (which he had brought out from a drawer and was holding in his hand) is a write off because it's so old". I didn't understand what he meant, and asked him to show me the case on display, that I had been looking at, thinking that I know his inventory better than him. But no, he shook his head and indicated that he could give me the phone case in his hand for free as it was a write off!

So, does it make sense to ask why did it happen to me (as we usually ask when something unpleasant happens)?

How did I attract this outcome? I was not high on the emotional scale and as we all know, good things only happen when we are high on the emotional scale?

Does it really matter why it happened as long as it did happen and as long as it was a positive outcome?

The only things I did were, 1) coming to terms with my near future situation of not having a case for my phone, and 2) just I had just left the chiropractor's office and got some relief for my aching hip. Yes, two small changes which don't change my situation much in the overall scheme of things. BUT, enough to cause a good and very positive thing to show up unexpectedly. It is surprising to me that two little things can cause an immediate positive shift in what happens, but I am beginning to understand that that is what the Law of Attraction is all about.

It shows good things are coming to me! It isn't it beautiful?!

A note from the Universe:
When you don't worry and fuss about things they happen easily? And when you worry about something it gets stuck and cannot change? You see, the Universe wanted to guide you out of the situation you created because of which you were in this place of anxiety. This is your personal proof that if you treat this and any other problem like you treated the replacement of your phone case and didn't make a big hairy deal of it then all things in your life would work out with ease and flow, for when you stop trying you allow the Universe free reign. The Universe has the ability to open all doors for you; the doors that you can see and the ones you cannot see, and even the ones you think are locked, for the Universe has the keys to them all. The Universe loves you no matter what decisions you make in life and will give you all the keys as soon as you step out of the way and into trust.

From a single Mom to a Bride - How I manifested my Husband

By Daniela Darling

Are you feeling lonely?
Do you want a loving relationship?
Have you dreamed of having a family since you were little?

If you hear your internal voice saying "yes", then continue reading; this is for you. While reading my story, you will feel pumped and excited because you are about to learn how to manifest the love you want.

There I was, living in a two-bedroom apartment with my child, my dog, and a male roommate, sharing one bathroom. I was feeling petrified as it was my first time having a roommate, a stranger, that I met while searching for an apartment online.

But on top of that, I was feeling devastated. I wanted a family so badly and felt that now I would have to give up that dream. I had to learn how to be a single mom, go back to school, and through it all keep myself motivated when all I wanted to do was cry. I couldn't even do that because I didn't want my little princess daughter to see me cry. I had to be strong for her and for me.

The silent pain continued when I did not have my child for Thanksgiving and I didn't feel like going to other families' homes. It was hard to process being alone on my 40th birthday, and alone again on Christmas, spending my day in bed, with Romeo, my dog, the only loyal creature in my life. My family is in Chile, so I chatted with them like everything was alright, but it wasn't. I felt like I had a hole in my chest.

My soul was searching, so I decided to try something new. I went to Vipassana, a meditation retreat for ten days where you don't talk to anybody. Someone I met there gave me the book "Conversations with God". Holy crap, this was the beginning of my real spiritual journey. Then my inner voice walked me to the bookstore, and following my intuition, I got many books, one of them was The Magic by Rhonda Byrne. (Get that book) I learnt the real deal about Thankfulness from that book. Start listening to your intuition, my friend. (If you don't have a clue where to start go to my website www.danieladarling.com, where you will find lots of free material to get you started.)

I wrote 900 sentences of thankfulness. Oh, babe, do it, and you will see Magic, my darling. Here is the secret: free up an evening to be alone. Prepare your favorite drink, incense, candle, music, a robe; feel comfortable and joyful. Buy yourself a gift, get the food you love, and sit with your notebook. Now start to write everything that you dream of, the ideal love of your life.

I wrote; he has completed the Landmark forum; he is family-oriented, plays piano, loves hiking, is a dog lover, has nice legs, tall and honest. I even mentioned the dimensions of his intimate part: affectionate kisses, and most importantly, a beautiful heart.

No kidding, he showed up exactly that way, but he

didn't knock on my door just like that. I tried online dating, oh yeah, I got bold and put myself out there. I dated a prosecution lawyer who pursued me big time but broke my heart. Still, I rose again from the ashes, and I was matched with Brian, he was the last one on my list, but God showed me a sign that he was the one. On our first date, we didn't kiss, but he told me everything, including his flaws.

After the daddy of my daughter, I never introduced her to anybody. I was afraid, but I was doing something new with Brian, so I stepped outside my comfort zone. My daughter said to me, "uh, he likes you!" Me; "yeah, I know, but I don't know if it will work". She said, well if it doesn't work, you just break up with him. Kaylee (5 years old)

Six months later, he got transferred to Washington. To make the story short, we broke up; my heart was in pieces, and while I was crying, I started to pray with all my heart. I got down on my knees and prayed out loud, please, if he is the love of my life, please God bring him back. I worshiped at my church, and I asked God to heal my wounds and envisioned Brian and me together. I believed it before I saw it. Three days later, he was suddenly notified that he got transferred back to San Diego. We got engaged on January 4, 2020.

And then Covid arrived, and you don't have to try very hard to imagine why 50% of divorces happened in 2020. It was cruel and caused hardship, fights, and many problems between us. I gained more weight than I have in my entire life and got stuck because my business stopped growing; my self-esteem decreased, and Brian became too hard to love. God is the only one besides Romeo and Kaylee to tell me not to give up.

Brian is younger than me, and he wants kids, while I'm not getting any younger. But we believed in the story of Abraham and Sarah and that anything is possible. My faith was tested once again when he broke up with me. Later that night, he was out and sent me a text message, "let's wait until Sunday to decide, lets go to the altar to pray for us and receive guidance". I prayed every day. I visualized morning and evening, feeling our civil wedding ceremony taking place.

What is amazing and shows how God works is that that day the sermon was about the story of Abraham and Sarah, and how Sarah gave birth to Issac when she was 90 and then the pastor called Brian and me to the altar and prayed with us, putting his hand on Brian's heart. The sign was clear. All doubts disappeared. We both knew that God was speaking to us. The guidance we had asked for was clear as day.

On July 29, 2021, I become Mrs. Darling.

A note from the Universe:
Appreciation is the most powerful force in the entire Universe. The vibration of appreciation is very close to the vibration of love. Everything you want becomes manifest at the vibration of love. When you put your trust in God/the Universe, despite all the reasons that tell you that you should not have what you want, then all the obstacles on your path disappear. Remember: *All things are possible*. Just because you cannot see a way for it to be, does not mean that a way does not exist.

Guidance is always being given to you, but a shift is required in order to learn how to understand it. When you feel bad about a situation, that does not mean that the thing you are intending is not for you or that it will not come about. What it means is that you are looking at things in a way that Source is not looking at them, so you need to change your perspective in order to manifest what you want. Even though the odds seemed against your union, but you choose the perspective of Source through visualization. You choose to believe that all things are possible despite the odds. That is what trust and faith are all about. Everything works the same way. Believe it, and then you will see it.

Things are always working out for me

By Felica Fleming

I decided to stop at the mall not too far from my house before heading into the city to shop. I got out of the car and as I was walking to enter the mall...I discovered my wallet was missing. I said let me re-trace my steps. Nothing. So, I said let me check the car. I called my friend...because he'd dropped me off and gone to get gas. I asked him to see if I left my wallet in the car. He looked but couldn't find it. He brought the car back so I could look for myself. I searched the car...NO WALLET!! Then I said...take me to the house and let me check there, even though I knew clear as day that I put that wallet in my pocket, before I left. I checked everywhere...knowing that at times I place things absentmindedly. Still, no wallet...checked outside no wallet. I had all my credentials from my job…pass code card, credit cards and a large sum of money. It was going to be a nightmare to replace everything…and the cash, there's no getting that back. I took a minute to breathe then I said to myself nothing is lost...I will find it...I let go and let God. Then I continued with my day. We went to the city as we had planned. When we returned home that evening I looked again, both outside and through the house. Still no wallet.

There was nothing to do...so I said a prayer to God...I said I remember all the times you never failed me. And I know everything will work out for me even if I don't feel it or see it. Then I let it go. The next day I was getting ready for work...and thinking that I would have to explain how I lost my credentials to my supervisor. My friend went out side...then approximately 5 minutes later...he came back in and gave me a hug...and he displayed a SOAKED wallet, my wallet! He found it in the street with all my credentials and money inside...and let me tell you...this wallet had a bright red 3 on it, so if you were walking you would surely find it. You see I have evidence now that everything is working out for me and God the Universe has my back.

A note from the Universe:
When you think something is lost, it cannot be found, because the Law of Attraction will bring you what you think. So as long as you keep thinking that something is lost, Law of Attraction will keep perpetuating it's loss. But when you give up, then the feeling of loss goes away and is replaced by acceptance. Acceptance is the willingness to move on despite the loss. For nothing is ever lost – the Universe always knows where everything is. Every blade of grass is known, every mustard seed is known, and therefore nothing is ever lost. It is just not visible to you.

Your desire to get your wallet back was never diminished. When you moved from the feeling of loss to the feeling of acceptance and giving up, now the Law of Attraction could respond to your desire instead of responding to the feeling of loss. This is why giving it over is such a powerful thing to do. For as long as you keep trying to get something that you think is lost or unavailable then the Law of Attraction cannot match you up with it.

The more we trust the easier it gets

By Gabriella Cassano

In June of 2010 we were on a hunt for a mobile home rental in Florida. My husband and I were retiring in January of 2011 and we planned to be away for the first month of retirement. We asked our friends, who owned a trailer in Bonita Springs Florida, to help find us a rental in their trailer park. After 4 months of looking they were unsuccessful. I decided to ask the Universe to help with this, so I put my search on hold for a few days, and let the Law of Attraction put me on a path.

A friend suggested I try searching the internet on "Vacation Rentals by Owners". I found an ad for a 1-1/2 bed mobile home in Naples, Florida, 20 minutes away from our friends'. The owner happened to live in Mississauga, an hour away from our Canadian home, and he invited us to his home to make the arrangements.

He and his wife were very welcoming, they too stayed in the trailer park at a second mobile home they owned. We stayed the month of January in the trailer, our landlord took us under their wing like family, often taking us out for breakfast and giving tips for getting around the area. We did have some issues; we discovered the mobile home was too small to have any of our children visit us and we didn't like being in a mobile park. We loved the Naples area and decided that next year we wanted to come back again to Naples, however we wanted to rent a condo instead. Before returning to Canada, we needed to find a condominium to stay in that had 2 bedrooms.

We checked newspaper ads, post-it boards in department stores all without success. Again, it was time to call on a Higher Power. I abandoned the search for a few weeks and one day while at the Costco in Naples, Florida The Law of Attraction put me on a path. There was a woman shopping in the aisle, and something came over me. I walked up to her, introduced myself and asked if she happened to live in Florida full time. Bingo! she did. She also happened to live in a condominium complex in Naples. I asked if she knew of anyone looking to rent in her complex. She told me her name was Dotty and she was the President of her Condominium Association. She handed me her phone number and asked me to call her when I was ready to look for a unit. I knew the Law of Attraction was guiding me and the best for us was on its way.

I waited a couple of days, and on a Saturday made the call. Dotty and her husband arranged to meet us at her condo complex to take us around. She walked with us from building to building as we made the phone calls for the listings posted on the buildings, but we got zero response. We had now spent the better part of the morning going from building to building. We were standing near the tennis court area at a bulletin board, as we thank her for her help. I told her that I was sure that the right condo for us would show up.

At this precise moment a woman was walking past us who heard me talking and stopped to ask if we were looking to rent a condo in the complex. She asked us to follow her, and took us to a condo she owned. This isn't just any condominium, it happens to have the view of the 2nd largest pool in southwest Florida which just happens to be in this complex. As we entered the unit my jaw dropped. It was the most beautiful condo ever. It was totally renovated, ceramic floors, new kitchen, a 4-poster bed, I couldn't believe it. The price was exceptionally reasonable, I turned to my husband and whispered to him to go to the car and grab our cheque book. We were not leaving without a contract signed. We enjoyed the whole month in Florida at that condo so much we decided to renew a two month contract for next year. The following year we spent 3 months at the same condo.

Now we were so enjoying our winters in Florida, I began thinking about what it would be like to own a condo in this complex, facing the pool of course. My husband and I began discussing the possibilities and both of us agreed we would only consider buying one if the condo available faced the pool. I began looking at a real estate website for the area and nothing was showing up. I never gave up my dream, time for the Universe to help with this. I left it for a couple of weeks and one day I grabbed my iPad while sitting at the pool. On the website there was just one listing for a condo in this complex on the pool side, and it was in our budget. Thank you, Universe! We called right away, made an appointment to view it the next morning, and by the next evening we had a signed contract to purchase the condo. We later found out that there were 4 people who were putting together offers to purchase just as we received the signed contract back. The Law of Attraction coordinated beautifully.

The Law of Attraction, for me, is a knowing - my belief the best for me will happen WHEN the Universe knows I am ready for it. I was skeptical early in my life, but many experiences have shown me how wonderful the Universe is to collaborate with me in experiencing Joy in my life.

A note from the Universe:
One thing leads to another, leads to another. You were already in a place of alignment when you birthed your desire to be in Florida and so only the best of things could come to you. As your desire became clearer to you, you knew exactly what you wanted and you came to the emphatic decision that you were ready to purchase a condo, the path started opening up. Combine that with a lack of attachment to the outcome and only the best of things can happen.

Most people are not really clear about what they want. They kinda sorta know what they want but it is a fuzzy picture, and so they end up manifesting what represents a mixed bag – some of what they do want and some of what they don't want. The best formula for manifesting quickly and easily is to be absolutely clear about what you want without attachment to it. Many people have clarity about what they want – they know exactly who they want to marry or exactly the job or business they wish to own, but their desire is accompanied by a very deep sense of attachment. They feel that they will miss out on the "opportunity" for ultimate happiness if they do not get this mate or this job. In doing so, they adopt an attitude of "lack". They think that there is only one thing that will make them happy, where as the Universe is abundant and at any given time there are scores of options that would be equally satisfying.

When you keep wanting to open just one door while you are attached to the thing that is on the other side of it, it is literally like pulling with all your might, while at the same time putting your knee in it with all your strength. In other words you start working against yourself and this is why you get stuck. The number one thing that keeps humans away from the manifestation of their desires is "attachment to the outcome". Believe in the abundance of the Universe.

You will know that you have attachment to the outcome if you are asking for the same thing over and over again. Ask and let it go, move on with an attitude that says, *"I care, but not that much"*. Caring is a good thing, but when you care so much that you stop moving forward then you become unhappy and when you are unhappy you cannot manifest what you want. Remember: *Abundance is your birthright*. An attitude of abundance means knowing that there is not just one opportunity, but an endless stream of opportunities to pick from.

Figuring out how to manifest

By Gay Merrill

I had a work contract that ended in March 2020, and I decided to take some time to work on several personal projects (writing two books and developing my cartoon drawing skills). I was also trying to decide what I would like my next work opportunity to be while living on my savings. I wasn't sure that I wanted to go back into the job market and still do the thing that I had been doing before – the idea did not excite me at all. So even though I wanted to find work, I wasn't sure what to look for. The year sped by, and when 2021 came along, panic set in as I realized my savings were dwindling. I needed to find work sooner rather than later. Like pronto.

I tried to use the Law of Attraction to manifest an opportunity, but I was feeling outside my comfort zone in turning it over to the universe. I hadn't reached a place of believing that things could be that easy – in other words, it sounded too easy to be true. My long held belief was that you first have to figure out what you want and then put all your energy into making it happen. But my thoughts around generating income through work were creating stress, and I got stuck in the "figuring it out" mode. Nothing was feeling good to me. Zehra's advice was to do what was easiest. For me what felt the easiest was work I was experienced in. She also advised me to go about finding work based on my beliefs and not to use strategies that went against my beliefs. She explained that we have to change our beliefs and buy into our new beliefs one hundred percent before we start taking action that corresponds to our new belief system. I knew what that meant – I wanted the process of finding work to be easy, but I didn't really believe that it could be easy. I believed it was hard work finding a job so of course the Law of Attraction would not make it easy for me.

To make things worse, I also didn't believe in using job banks or head hunters – I didn't trust the system, and I felt like my application would just get swallowed into a dark hole. One day I had a thought that I should try out LinkedIn. I trusted that platform more than any others, so I set up notifications for the type of work I was already experienced in. That strategy did get me a job interview for an opportunity that looked interesting. I didn't get the job though and was relieved as I didn't have a great feeling from the interview about the work and the hiring manager.

After much trial and error and listening to Law of Attraction videos related to finding work, I decided to focus on keeping myself in a higher vibration by doing things I enjoy. I returned to my book projects and daily drawing practice along with walking. "The universe has my back" was my mantra. I kept telling myself that the Universe knew what I wanted and now all I had to do was to wait for it to unfold. As a result of this decision, I started feeling better, even though nothing else had really changed.

It wasn't too long after that decision I received two different inquiries for my services. They came to me! As opposed to my working hard to get noticed by them. This was so different from anything I had experienced before. I wound up accepting a contract working for a well known social media company, with people who are super nice, doing work I enjoy and earning more than my previous contracts.

Now I have my own personal proof that the Law of Attraction does work, and I am excited about all the changes that are possible in my life because of it.

A note from the Universe:
It is a human tendency to think that you have to "give, in order to get", whereas in reality the only thing you have to give is your appreciation. You were born worthy and deserving of all good things, and you do not need to prove your worthiness or earn your right to receive what you desire. In fact, your belief that you need to earn your right to things you want is actually a hinderance because it leads you to compare yourself with others. "Other people are more skilled than I am", "those others have connections", "what if my resume isn't written properly and theirs is", and so on. When you compare you either find fault with yourself or with someone else – either way the vibrational frequency that you land on is negative, because neither of those two options feels good. Good things cannot come from thoughts that feel bad. As a result you get caught in a sort of holding pattern because Law of Attraction will find things that will lead to the perpetuation of the vibration.

When you made the conscious decision to repeat the mantra "the Universe has my back" you reintroduced your worthiness into your thinking, and so Law of Attraction had no choice to bring you results that matched this new vibration.

Often people think that big changes or sacrifices have to be made when the "stakes are high" or something that is important to you is involved, but it not so. A small shift in the way you think and feel can generate widely different results.

Everything works the same way, and so because you now have your own results, you can use them as a reminder that helps you to create the shift that will assist you in moving forward in a better feeling way with manifestations that show you clearly that you are heading in the right direction.

Remember: *You are Unlimited, you can have, be or do anything you want.*

An immigrant's dream

By Hannah Ghazanfar

Everyone told me I was crazy, but I knew I had to do something to secure the future for myself and my children. I had to gamble everything. It was now or never.

I have to say one thing to credit my husband; he always speaks his mind, but even when he disagrees with me, he always supports me one hundred percent once a decision is made. We were at a deadlock. I was for – he was against. I could see his point of view, but I also knew that the risk would be worth it – something in the pit of my belly told me that I should trust and move forward.

We were considering purchasing the Master franchise for the territory of Quebec for Nhance. Given the fact that Quebec is a French speaking province and we only know how to say merci, the idea sounded preposterous not only to my husband but also to others whom we approached for advice.

My husband and I had relocated ourselves and our four kids to Ontario from Pakistan. We knew that it wouldn't be easy to start over, but we wanted a to bring our family up in a safer environment and so my husband and I both gave up lucrative careers and pulled the plug on everything. It took us almost two years of exploring while we used up our savings to finally give up trying to go back into corporate life. We decided to start exploring small business opportunities and finally signed up for a franchise with Nhance in 2018.

We had never operated a business like this before. Talk about going from sitting behind a desk to making the desk! Yikes!!! Yes, we bought a woodworking franchise specializing in kitchens and floors. I packed up my business attire and went shopping for track suits!

We were hungry to grow our business as quickly as possible and so we would take on all sorts of jobs big or small, close or far. We didn't care. As long as we could clear some money, we were game. Slowly but surely the results started coming in. We started feeling better about our odds for success. We thought of expanding our business by acquiring other territories, but none of the options were exciting enough. It was at a local lunch that were offered an opportunity to become a franchisor for the province of Quebec – French speaking Canada. We laughed it off – of course, we weren't going to Quebec.

The more I thought about it, the more I felt that this was an opportunity and MUST seize it. Who cares if we don't speak French. If we can cross the oceans to come to a new country, we can surely go to another province in the same country? So what if we didn't speak French? You see, I had travelled and done business with countries whose language I could not speak, in my corporate life. "People who speak all sorts of languages do business with each other – it can't be all that hard." I said.

It was the latter half of 2020, we had to sign up or give up. Many discussions and sleepless nights ensued. It wasn't just about acquiring the Master franchise, it was about coming up with the financing arrangements, developing the corporate infrastructure, learning the culture and the laws, for as we soon discovered Quebec is labelled as a Canadian province but for all intents and purposes it is a world unto itself. I knew that if we did this, we would have to act fast, because we would be squeezing every drop of available finances to make this possible.

The little voice inside me nudged me on. I trusted it and my family trusted me.

It just so happened that in January of 2021, just a few days prior to signing the contract a friend happened to visit. Not only did she support our decision, but she promised to introduce us to a few people she knew who lived in Quebec and may be able to assist us in getting started. This was literally a God send. We were introduced to Karine, who became our trusted representative in Quebec and was instrumental in helping us sign our very first franchisees.

As I look back now, I can see the series of events that took place and recognize the role that trust played in the unfolding. God/the Universe showed me my next step and I said "yes". I believe that this was the reason that at every juncture, the right people showed up to help me to continue moving forward. We are celebrating the completion of our first year of business in Quebec, and I am beyond grateful for the divine guidance that has helped us create a thriving business. I am excited about all the opportunities that are waiting to unfold for us as well as our franchisees in the future.

Nhancequebecfranchise.ca
hannah.g@nhancequebecfranchise.ca

A note from the Universe:
Trust is the theme of this story. Hope comes from trusting that we have divine help, therefore even though we cannot see the future, we can move forward fearlessly.

It takes trust to move from one country to another. It takes trust to find work and build a new life. It takes trust to build something out of nothing.

Trust is what brings Universal forces to play on our behalf. When we doubt and question, we stall our progress forward towards the things we want.

Birthday celebration

By Jennifer Piscione

I have always loved and adored my Birthday! With that said, I always found myself sad and disappointed on my Birthday. The usual thoughts were, "Is everyone going to be busy and not show up to celebrate?" "Will I feel special?" "Is this Birthday going to be unsatisfying like it normally is?" Thinking these thoughts never felt good, yet it had become a habit to think in such negative ways. Looking back, I see how my negative thoughts kept the momentum going of Birthdays that didn't go the best. The worry and sadness just made things worse and manifested the opposite of what I wanted.

In July 2020, I made a decision, and lined up with it! I said to myself, "This year can be different, I can make the best of my birthday and enjoy my special day!". I knew what this meant. It meant, I would have to change my self-talk - the voice in my head. Thankfully I was able to do that with all I have learnt from Zehra about the Law of Attraction.

I made a pact with myself, no matter what is going on, I would celebrate my Birthday! I thought to myself, this year is going to be better than any other year. I chose to be happy, I had learned enough about the Law of Attraction to know that the way things would turn out was all up to me and my ability to remain positive. The word celebrate was active in my vibration. I decided even if no one is available and I am on my own, I would have fun and celebrate. I thought of what could go right, instead of what might go wrong, I focused on what I like rather than what I do not like. I could get a cake, candles, balloons, decorations and even treat myself to dinner. I even had fun thinking "I will have a pretty cake, what am I going to pick to have for dinner? I love decorations and balloons!" My thought process did a 360. It felt so much better, the thoughts I was now thinking were serving me well, because even though nothing had changed, I felt better. I didn't make any plans, I let it go, knowing that it was possible to have a good birthday.

Well, for the first time in my life, I didn't just have a good birthday, I had a great birthday. In fact, I had three birthday celebrations. I was showered with beautiful gifts; I received three cakes and had the most enjoyable, and very special day.

Coincidence? I think not. I had let go of my past negative beliefs, I had let go of all resistance and let the Universe take over and plan out the details. I was open to allowing the Universe to surprise and delight me. The result was magnificent. It solidified my knowing that our thoughts are powerful, and that a little positive shift in our thoughts not only feels better but leads to amazing results. Looking back, I can see that I had become okay with the idea of celebrating alone. I had let go of attachment to the outcome and made room for the Universe to deliver me what I desired.

Now, I know what to do not just for my birthday, but for every important event in my life. Now, I know that my work is to find ways to think about it with positive anticipation and let the Universe do the rest.

A note from the Universe:
Humans misjudge time. Things don't have to take time unless you think they do. In the instant that you make a decision and then start thinking thoughts that support your decision, the direction of your future reality starts changing. Often, people make decisions, but do not make a shift in the way they are thinking. Remember: *a new decision requires a new way of thinking that supports your decision and reinforces it, in order for your future to reflect your decision.*

Your success was brought about by your making a new decision and following it through with thoughts that were different compared to the way you used to think in the past. Your manifestations reflected it! This is the meaning of alignment. *Think thoughts that support your end goal.* When you fuss and worry you think thoughts that oppose what you want to manifest, or you think some thoughts that support and some that oppose – which results in a split vibration, literally pulling you apart. That is why people who worry feel as if they are being pulled apart – because they are.

Manifesting a miraculous rendezvous with my childhood idol

By C. Jill Hofer

What did you want to be when you grew up? As a little kid on a small midwestern farm, I'd stare at the beautiful mermaid on the tuna can as it sat on the kitchen counter above my eye-level. Mom would let me hold the can before she opened it and I'd dream of the mermaid life. I'd wear a sparkly blue sweetheart cut dress and live with my underwater friends in an adventurous life under the sea. My magic star wand would grant all the wishes and my long flowing blond hair would have a bun up top.

Later, as an adult, I have the hair and the bun, plus plenty of sparkly blue mermaid outfits for fire dancing at the Tucson Mermaid Parade. I even have a jewelry company with a star as my signature, bringing magic to clients and granting wishes to the nonprofits receiving donations from my jewelry. As far as childhood dreams go, I'd say close enough! But it turns out there was more in store.

Enjoying my journey as a jewelry designer, I created the first Braille jewelry line. I collaborated with an organization serving people with low vision and there I met Syd Berger, an artist who painted expansive, colorful canvasses. I added Braille beads to her canvasses so her fellow individuals with low vision could "feel" evocative phrases in Braille depicting the feelings, colors and emotions of her art.

Syd, who was probably 30 years my senior, once asked, "Honey, what did you want to be when you grew up?" It was a question I had NEVER answered honestly. But for some reason, this time I followed an impulse to tell the truth and I'm so glad I did.

I ignored the resistant thoughts that a smarter sounding answer would be better. I bluntly and honestly proclaimed "I wanted to be the mermaid on the tuna can." Syd's face dropped in shock and surprise. She didn't say a word. Instead she stood up, turned around and walked to a cabinet. I saw her pull out a dusty old scrapbook. She sat down next to me, opened the book and turned to a full page spread with photos and news clippings of her experience POSING AS THE MODEL FOR THE MERMAID ON THE CAN.

Was that my manifestation, hers, or a co-creation of BOTH? Definitely both!

Check out Jill's jewelry designs on her website: https://aniceworld.com/home/

A note from the Universe:
The Universe never forgets.

When you wish for something, you may forget it, but the Universe never deletes your request. Whenever there is an opportunity to bring you things that you once wished for, that would still make you happy the Universe will do so. You see, when you forget a desire, you also forget all the reasons it cannot be – and for that very reason, it must be.

Plus, the Universe enjoys bringing you surprises to communicate with you. When you are heading in the right direction, the Universe brings you surprises that confirm your alignment – like orchestrating a meeting with the mermaid that was special to you in your childhood. When you are out of alignment the Universe brings you the evidence of your direction of thought so that you can recalibrate your thoughts.

Remember: *All desires are valid, and do not need justification.*

A path to greater real estate success

By C. Jill Hofer

The story of how I came to be the owner and caretaker of multiple properties has many chapters, twists, turns and tales of Law of Attraction in action. It all started with attending a Buddhist Tozo (chanting session). I am a member of SGI Buddhism, the branch focused on Law of Attraction. When my host said "Come back in 20 minutes with evergreen for the altar," I drove around the area looking for a pine tree or rosemary bush. In 10 minutes I found the street of my dreams, where we now own three homes and one beautiful natural open lot.

Fast forward to 2019 and I follow my impulse to book a spot on the Abraham Hicks Alaskan Cruise – what a life event! At the time I had two other rentals which had recently become vacant, an oddity for me. I knew I could get them rented fast before the ship sailed, or I could REALLY trust the Law of Attraction and see what happened if I delayed listing them by 3 weeks due to the cruise timing. I decided to trust the universe. "OK Law of Attraction!" I said, "Let me see you do your stuff!"

Fast forward 1 week, I'm at the City Hostel in Seattle meeting my incredible "roommate match" April. Turns out – along with a half a million other things we have in common – she ALSO owns rental properties. I explained that I was holding my breath but expecting the best for big shifts during the cruise. Her response? "Girl, hand me your phone."

One hour later I am enrolled as a landlord on Furnished Finder. One day later I have house #1 rented. Three days later I have house #2 rented, both to 13-week Travel Nurses who are pre-screened, have great incomes, super can-do attitudes who will be in, out, done and happy. One week later I am shopping for fun, interesting, welcoming furnishings with a warm, local feel.

Thanks to April and the Law of Attraction, I am now a professional dollhouse player, with life sized doll houses and real living dolls who are happy, content and comfortable, loving where they live. And to top it off with the icing on the cake – April is the person who introduced me to ZEHRA. The gift that keeps on giving! Love it.

A note from the Universe:
You followed your emotional guidance system at every juncture; that is exactly how it's supposed to be. When you identify what you want and allow the Universe to chart the course, and just look for your next step; life becomes easy. There is never any need for struggle. When you trust your guidance, then the Universe can show you the way, and all you have to do is to follow along. Unfortunately, most people try to create the path themselves instead of following the path that is unfolding in front of them. There is no struggle in this way of living, and it is effortless and fun.

Remember: *Your success is certain when you trust that the Universe will show you the way.*

A rollercoaster ride

By Karine Morin

Life was tough, as a single mom with four little boys under the age of 6 and no work. The emotional turmoil created by my separation led me to resigning a highly paid job, and I decided that I needed a fresh start so I took the boys and moved to a new city, 12 hours away from my support network of friends and parents. I was asking the Universe for help and trusting that somehow things would work out – though at that time I did not know how. The I discovered the Law of Attraction on YouTube and everything changed.

My journey started when I came across Zehra Mahoon on YouTube. All the things she was teaching were resonating with me. I decided to buy the book Unlimited 40 days workout and started following Zehra on Facebook.

It took me time to clean out the clutter in my mind as I realized very early on that everything depended upon my self-talk and listening to my emotions. I immersed myself in listening to Zehra on YouTube and Facebook, because it was very important for me to understand more and continue my spiritual growth. When Zehra decided to create the Unlimited 365 group where she is live everyday, I was so happy and excited that I subscribed immediately! The daily teachings in this group really helped me to go up the emotional scale and become balanced in my ability to maintain my vibration! It took about 7 months of daily teachings for me to obtain a stability and start manifesting happy things! My biggest manifestation is certainly the one for my work.

I found some part-time work, but it was barely sufficient to scrape by. I wanted something more suitable which would pay better and still give me flexibility of being able to look after my boys. I put my wish out to the Universe and let it go. Within a few months I found a better job and was able to rent an apartment as well as make daycare arrangements for my boys that were only a short walk from home. Things were beginning to fall into place. I was happy.

An important shift that happened for me was that I started to think differently about my ex. As a result, my relationship with him began to improve and he started to help me with some of the responsibilities of looking after the boys.

Just a few months later, on 1st of January 2021, the Universe brought me another opportunity to help with the setting up of a new franchise business in the province of Quebec.

At that time, I had a sales job at Telus, a cellular company, and was doing really well. By now I knew the power of appreciation, and I had manifested a great team of people to work with. The management was super accommodating towards me and the chances for growth within the company looked really good. I took on the franchise work on the side for extra money, but it soon became clear that my employers wanted me to put in more than just a few hours a week. I had a decision to make – stay with Telus or jump head long into this new company. I think most people would have told me that I should stay with Telus which was an established company rather than work for a new company without any track record, but I allowed my heart to guide me.

I had no idea how a franchise worked and I did not know anything about the industry and the products that this franchise offered, but I said to myself that everything is possible and no matter what job I am doing, because I am great and fantastic person, I will do great and fantastic job!

It did not take me long to start excelling at my new job, and I started really enjoying working with my new employer. I became instrumental to helping establish all the systems and procedures for this new company and helped with the sale of 4 franchises, within a record period of just four months.

On the 7th of August, I received a surprise. I had been thinking of asking my employer for a raise and I had a certain figure in mind. You know what? I received the exact amount I wanted without even asking! I was very impressed, and it confirmed to me that we get what we expect!

Fast forward to March of 2022, I received an excellent bonus at work and decided to take the opportunity to strike it out on my own. For a while, I had been feeling that there is a need for teaching business owners how to use the Law of Attraction for business and personal success. I had even coached the franchisees and our business partners informally from time to time over the last few months, and I feel a strong pull to trust that it was time for me to create something of my own. And so, at the time of the writing and publication of this book, I have established my company to begin offering in-depth Law of Attraction training the French language in Quebec using Zehra's books and programs as the basis for my work.

If you are interested in finding out more about my work feel free to connect with me on social media.

A note from the Universe:
You applied yourself to the goal of becoming the best version of you. You immersed yourself in understanding how the Universe works. You did not treat the fact that you were a single mom with young children as a disadvantage, instead you used it as an impetus to find a way forward.

The secret to your success is the belief that "all things are possible" (trust in the Universe) and that "I am a fantastic person and capable of fantastic work regardless of the subject matter" (trust in yourself). This is in fact, a winning formula that makes all things possible.

The best part about it is that once you test this formula and you see how it works, you are able to use it for all situations in your life. Your life becomes full of possibilities and all things you want and need come to you. Remember: *you don't need to prove anything to anyone, all you have to do is to remain open to new ways of thinking and doing.*

A Miraculous Reunion

By Kat Rodriguez

During high school, I met a very special friend. We became pretty inseparable after meeting in a class one day. We did everything together. We ditched school a whole bunch of times to go eat, watch movies, or go shopping. We helped each other quite a bit in those days. He showed me how to enjoy the finer things in life and simply have fun. I helped him acknowledge that he is gay and even introduced him to the first boy he kissed. Being gay in the 90s was not easy, but I was lucky enough to be with him during that time. His coming out taught me how important and brave it is to be your authentic self. I believe I was also questioning my sexuality during that time, but I had not come to terms with it just yet. I remember we would visit bookstores and speed walk straight to the gay section. We would giggle and blush while we flipped through the pages with such innocence and curiosity.

We had great fun crossing the border from El Paso, Texas into Juárez, Mexico. We frequented many clubs and danced all night. One night, we couldn't get into one of our favorite clubs because they were having a wedding. We went up to the door anyways and lied our little teeth off. I told the bouncer that our names were on the list. I threw out the first names that came to mind and announced us as Maria and Jose. Bouncer looked at his list, checked our names, and allowed us entry! We ate cake, danced, toasted to the bride, and had so much fun. We later laughed and vowed that we would get married to each other by the time we reached 30 if we were still single.

We took our first big trip together to San Francisco. We relished in fine dining, credit card maxing at Saks, and watching our very first opera, Phantom of the Opera. We visited Castro Street and lost our little minds. I remember taking his picture while he delightfully saluted the rainbow flag. We walked all over the city and dreamed of what type of people we wanted to be when we got older.

After graduation, he moved away for college and I moved to Los Angeles to study fashion design at the Fashion Institute of Design and Merchandising. We kept in touch and visited each other whenever we could, which wasn't much. Upon graduating college, he came to visit me and we picked up right where we left off. It seemed appropriate to celebrate the moment as well as our friendship by racing to Sunset Boulevard where we got our first tattoos together.

As we got older and worked on our careers, time passed and we saw less and less of each other. Upon one of our visits, we slowly realized how different we had become. We wound up getting into an awful fight. I flew back home feeling so upset. Days went by and we didn't talk. Days turned into weeks and weeks turned into months and months turned into years. I would periodically get the itch to call and apologize, but I didn't. I felt that he was probably happy to have me out of his life.

I recently learned that my friend was back in our hometown to be with family during the pandemic. I saw on social media that he was hanging out with a mutual friend of ours. I felt such a sense of loss as I looked at the pictures of them hiking and wished I could join them. I wanted to reach out to our mutual friend and ask if he ever asked about me. Instead, I got extremely saddened thinking he must never want to hear from me again.

I then started to think about all of our good times together. I wondered how his life must be like now. I wondered if he had found love. I wondered if we would ever see each other again and if we did how would it be? I then imagined seeing him in person and getting all the answers to my questions. Scenes of us laughing and hugging each other came to mind. I let go of my sadness, wished him well, and returned to my desk to work.

Three hours later, I saw a text come through. I took a quick glance and could not believe what I was reading. It was my friend! He said he was travelling to Tucson, AZ to stay for the weekend and wanted to know if I wanted to see him. I could not believe what I was reading! I quickly replied that I would meet him anywhere. After 15 years of separation, we finally got to see each other. We laughed, cried, and talked through the early hours of the night. It was even better than what I had imagined. We both apologized and vowed that we wouldn't let a fight get in the way of our friendship again.

This special reunion with my friend reminded me just how powerful the Law of Attraction is. My circumstances were different this time because I envisioned what I did want versus what I didn't. I raised my vibration to tune into a higher frequency and then I let go of the outcome. Shifting to feeling good and happy about our friendship was the key that finally unlocked that door that had been shut all these years. After seeing my friend that night, I remember thinking on the drive home how spectacular the day had unfolded. My manifestation felt serendipitous and nothing short of a miracle.

A note from the Universe:
Letting go is the step before letting in. People often think that when they let go of something they want, that they are letting go the desire for it. That's not actually true. From the point of view of energy, once a desire is born it can never be taken back, because energy once it is created can only change form, it can never go away. So when we let go of something, we are not letting go the desire for it; we are letting go our attachment; we are letting go our negative beliefs, and when we do that then those negative things are no longer holding us back so now good things must come.

A little effort to let go the things that are upsetting and instead focusing on the things that we appreciate creates a big vibrational shift. You see, we think that when we want something that seems big, then we must do something big or commiserate in size and effort to "earn" it, but the reality is that a small emotional shift can result in what seem like big manifestations. This is because to the Universe, nothing is either big or small. Big things don't take any more energy to create and manifest as small things. That is why Abraham (Hicks) uses the phrase: *it is as easy to create a castle as a button*.

Deepak's Lecture

By Kat Rodriguez

I became interested in the Law of Attraction many years ago. I stumbled upon it during a time in my life where I felt quite lost. It happened while flipping through channels one night and coming across a PBS special with Wayne Dyer. Every word and principle he shared about the law of attraction naturally resonated with me. It felt like he was talking directly to me! I was eager to learn more about the subject and so I began to read all of his books.

As my desire to learn more grew, I eventually found Jerry and Esther Hicks, and of course, Abraham. My little mind was blown! Abraham became a huge deal for me and I devoured every word and teaching I came across. I learned next about Deepak Chopra and found love in his words as well. Throughout all my research, you can bet I was applying the law of attraction in my life. Sometimes I was successful and sometimes …not so much. However, I never stopped being curious.
I remember one day thinking how neat it would be to meet Deepak Chopra and hear him speak in person. The following week, I learned from my colleague that the University of Arizona was hosting a lecture with none other than Deepak Chopra! Deepak would be giving his lecture just down the street from where I work in just a few days. I mean…seriously?! I was so amazed! I was not sure how I had missed that information, but it didn't matter because I knew now. I moved fast to buy a ticket, but sadly it was sold out. I was so upset thinking I got so close and now I wasn't going to see him.

The day finally came when Deepak would be in town for his lecture. There was a buzz circulating over this event. I went out for lunch feeling so depressed, but I eventually let go. I envisioned myself in the crowd with a big smile on my face while I heard him speak. I imagined the feeling you get when you feel lucky. I could even feel the goosebumps on my arms from the sheer delight of all that magic. When I returned from lunch, my colleague informed me that he was stepping out to raffle tickets to Deepak's lecture. At the time, I worked as a marketing specialist for an academic hospital and we worked closely with the University of Arizona. I remember I was dying to show interest and just point blank beg him for a ticket, but I didn't. I let go once again and envisioned the winners of those tickets being so happy that they won. Imagining their smiles and being happy naturally made me feel better.

As my day wrapped up, I got ready to leave my office. I then heard some noise in the back. It was my colleague. I asked him how his raffling turned out. He said it went great and that he had raffled out all tickets. I congratulated him and truly meant it and began to walk away. He then started telling me about how he didn't want to miss his son's soccer game, which was later that same night. He asked me if I could do him a favor and take his ticket to Deepak's lecture. I swiftly responded with a "sure, I can help you with that," but inside I was screaming like a 13 year old girl!

And just like that, I was sitting front and center at Deepak's lecture just one hour later and I was wearing the biggest smile you ever did see! I was filled to the brim with delight and a profound understanding of the law of attraction. Goosebumps rose all over me like little fist bumps in the air. It was similar to how I envisioned myself just a few hours earlier, but even better. I felt truly lucky as all the cells in my body percolated and danced in the midst of what felt like magic. I understood now how important it is to let go and detach from the outcome so you can trust in the universe and allow life to unfold.

A note from the Universe:
The two things that made the difference in what happened for you were that you were genuinely happy for the people who were going and they you could see yourself being one of them. Had you approached the situation with a feeling of jealously then your own success would have been hampered, for jealousy is a negative energy. In thinking that you are more deserving in comparison with another you look at other in a way that your Source does not agree with, for as far as your Source is concerned everyone is equally worthy. Jealously often feels like someone else is taking what should have been yours, but this is never true for each person creates for themselves, and no one else has access to it. When someone has what you want and you decide to appreciate them and their ability to create and allow, then by the powerful Law of Attraction you create and allow some of it in your own life. Being happy for others is one of the highest forms of love, and will always bring good feeling manifestations in your own life.
Remember: *how we think and feel about others is indicative of our own level of joy.*

Expecting good things, brings good things

By Lakshmi Balakrishnan

I have always been one who expects good things to happen. I had an awesome childhood. I manifested the best parents and siblings. I always thought my parents were making good decisions for me and I expected things to go well. When I got married, I expected things to go well and I recently celebrated my 38th wedding anniversary with my amazing husband. When I had children, I expected that they would be good kids and they are. And now I have a beautiful granddaughter who I absolutely adore. My whole life is a wonderful manifestation.

During the course of several years I have manifested jobs, computers, cars and homes and so much more. Migrating to Canada in itself was a major manifestation. Parking spots are a non-issue. I always get one with ease. All these came to me easily without much effort. But I did not know how this was happening to me or for me. When I was younger I assumed that is how everyone's life is and was. Now that I am learning about the Law of attraction I am beginning to understand a little more and deliberately applying the principles more consistently.

As I look back upon my life, I can see how the Law of Attraction brought us the things we asked for. Take the example of our immigration to Canada. There was civil and political unrest in Sri Lanka almost 40 years ago. During this time, we took refuge in a house that belonged to my husband's cousin, along with the families of other cousins. One day, one of the cousins asked my husband to drive him to the Canadian Embassy because he wanted to apply for immigration to Canada. When they spoke to an embassy official, his cousin was told that he was not eligible to apply, but it turned out that my husband was eligible, as his sister and husband lived in Canada, and they could sponsor us.

We had not considered immigration to Canada before this. Looking back, it feels as if the Universe was showing us a path because of our desire for a stable environment in which to raise our family. My husband thanked the official at the embassy and brought the application form home. We needed to attach documents to the form which we did not have with us since we were not in our home at that time, so we put the form away at the bottom of our luggage and forgot about it. Months later when things settled down and we returned to our home, I was unpacking the bag and I came across these forms, and we decided to apply for immigration to Canada. Once we did that we went about our lives once again and forgot about it. Within a very short time we got called for an interview and were asked to do our medicals. We both passed with flying colours and a few months later we received the necessary paperwork to enter Canada. Everything happened with ease and we both landed in Canada. We have been living happily in Canada for the past 38 years.

When I think about it now, I can see that my husband and I never made a big deal about leaving Sri Lanka, like other folks. We were happy then, and we would have been just as happy continuing to live there if the immigration had not been processed. Both of us have always had an attitude of acceptance and appreciation and as a result we have created an easy and abundant life.

Recently I have been asking the Universe to show me beautiful things and I am noticing that almost every time I go out for a walk I see incredibly beautiful sunsets, or flowers, or trees or Amazing cloud formations or the sun shining through the clouds in a particular way that is incredibly beautiful. Even looking out my window I have seen breathtaking sunsets, each one different from the others. I have taken many photographs of some of these on my phone.

Recently I have made contact with friends who I had not seen for 50 years and we are able to pick up as if we had been in touch all along.

Every day the Universe brings me things to appreciate. I have also started to appreciate myself more. I am often prompted to read something or listen to something. When I do follow my intuition, I see that is just what I needed to hear that day. I now know everything is working out for me and that all is well.

Life is simply awesome. I am extremely happy where I am and reaching for more.

A note from the Universe:
There is power in being general about your goals. There is power in having goals for the way you want to feel instead of goals that are about specific manifestations.

There is power in finding ways to accept the reality that has already manifested while being hopeful that the future will be better than the past. These are some of the things that have led to your success.

Your attitude of being forward thinking has created ease and flow in your life so that you are never far from being in a place of satisfaction. You have always established goals for yourself that seemed achievable even when they made you stretch. You made sure that the stretch did not create imbalance, so there has always been a sort of sureness in your movement forward, because it has helped you to maintain your emotional balance, enabling you to always say "yes, I can do it" or "we can do it together".

Many people dream of things that seem out of reach. As a result, it is much harder for them to say "yes, I can do it". Even as they reach forward they doubt their success. Remember: *doubt contradicts desire*.

I will never spend another holiday alone

By Lyndsay King

Have you ever looked at your life and realized that there is something so greatly out of alignment that it just seems too big to change, so beyond your control? Something that is so wrong with the way things have unfolded that you just can't see how it would ever be possible to change?

We are discussing the topic of manifestation in this book. And I am going to share a miraculous story that describes and illustrates my most recent miracle that I will stand up and take responsibility for manifesting in my own personal life. Through this example I hope to inspire your heart, dare you to take a chance to dream, want and desire all that you deserve even if you do not see the way, or even think there is a possibility.

My Manifestation

In 2019 I was in the midst of a massive awakening in my adult life. I was approaching 40 years old, a big birthday for me, living in London and having lived and travelled all over the world, had a successful career, and facing the truth about my life. I was single and never married. I was outgrowing London. And I was no longer interested in working as a consultant for my own company. Deeply I knew I needed a change.

By July of 2019 I had closed my business and decided to

run my "inspirational" side-business full time. I began hosting events speaking about energy and manifestation to inspirational women in business.

By November 2019, I had developed a methodology, the Accelerate Your Life Process. When I commenced as student within my own program I decided to raise the bar. With tears falling from my eyes one night in late November I declared that I was no longer accepting my existing life and I demanded a change. Not only was I commencing on a new journey in business but I was going to commit to manifesting the impossible.

I decreed that I would never spend another holiday (such as Christmas) on my own. Now for most this may seem a silly notion, who doesn't have family to visit on the holidays? Well not everyone, is the honest answer.

My family lived in the US and I had lived in the UK for over 13 years. In the US my immediate family was scattered across different states, and further to that not in good standing with one another.

The most immediate sign of a real result was when I had a call from an auntie in upstate NY announcing Christmas at her home that winter. Flights were terribly expensive and again I felt the defeat. A few days later I decided out of the blue to look for flights and found the most inconceivable deal and flew home for a wonderful Christmas holiday, the first I'd had in over a decade.

At that point I thought I had indeed manifested what I wanted and left it at that. Little did I know that the universe was at work behind the scenes.

When Covid hit in March of 2020 we had to relocate my father to my aunt's house temporarily. As the pandemic unfolded I suddenly awoke one night in mid-April with a voice in my head saying to hand in notice for my central London flat and move back to the US. I was stunned. But I trusted my guidance and listened and handed in my notice and booked the first flight out of London when the pandemic lockdown lifted at the end of May 2020. I flew back.

By chance the Friday before I was set to complete my quarantine, I started to look for apartments merely as a form of entertainment. I found a beautiful loft that strangely realizing later was on a vision board I had created many months earlier, and filled out an application and was approved. That morning we decided to move Dad in with me to alleviate my aunt of the long-term guest.

Let me fast forward. A few months later my mother moved into the same building complex (again the impossible), and currently me, my father and my mother are all living in the building community together, all in three different apartments. This has created a ripple effect of healing and unity throughout our family and brought all of us closer on both sides in ways no one could ever have imagined.

The moral of this story is this. Be careful what you wish for because when it shows up, it is important to take responsibility for what you are manifesting. The Universe will always swing into action and through changes out of your control will bring you what you want every time.

Now I know that not only will I never have another holiday alone without my family, but the family reunion has commenced and it's in full swing. Yes, it has its ups and downs, as all things do, but my life is currently full of exactly what I wanted. A full and vibrant daily life beyond possibility, beyond my wildest dreams. My family on such a large scale is uniting across the country, and more and more continues to unfold to bring us together. And to add to that, all of the other things I had been manifesting my life came along with the shift. This is what I like to call a quantum leap.

The leaps keep happening, my life is unfolding exactly the way I decree it to be, and all of it is out of my control, the how is up to the universe. The one thing that is in my control is the dream, the want, and the desire for what I choose.

About Lyndsay King
Lyndsay King Accelerate Your Life Academy
Lyndsay King is the creator of the Accelerate Your Life Coaching methodology and CEO of the Accelerate Your Life Academy, a global online school focused on supporting people in understanding energy transference, quantum physics and how to achieve breakthrough growth and transformation in both life and business. She has a 20+ year career in Communications and lived and travelled all over the world. As an entrepreneur Lyndsay has founded multiple businesses including Hourglass Inspiration, inspirational women in business, and SaveTheHighStreet.org in the UK. She speaks on stages

motivating corporate and conference audiences on mindset, success, and how to unlock potential and personal freedom. Lyndsay has been featured in the media, and appears on PodCasts regularly. She spends her free-time cycling, practicing yoga and fitness, hiking, horse riding, skiing, and reading.

A note from the Universe:
There is power in making a decision and lining up with it. Decisions move you forward, and you can begin to receive guidance that is specific to what you have decided. You made a very clear decision never to be alone on a holiday ever again.

Most people waffle. They decide one thing. Then they scrap that and make another decision. Remember: *Every thought counts, the Law of Attraction responds to every thought you think.* When you think a little bit of this and a little bit of that, you get a little bit of this and a little bit of that.

What I learned about Law of Attraction by missing my flight to Dubai

By Monisha Mittal

This story is actually two stories…the story of how I met Zehra and the story of what happened next.
I had dabbled with LOA over the years… before being married and after being married. Soon after I got married, I started getting deeper into it. I started practicing appreciation and gratitude journaling and started listening to Abraham Hicks on YouTube. I was always exploring and finding myself on websites to learning the terminology that Abraham uses like "momentum" and "up the hill" and "down the hill" and "the path of least resistance". Soon I found myself attracting Zehra as my coach. Coaching with her was a fabulous experience because she opened me up and gave me a much deeper dimension into Abraham and into what I was understanding and not understanding. One of the things I learnt to do from her was to pre-pave or set clear intentions and think positively.

I remember that around that time I was travelling to India via Dubai for a big family wedding (well, all Indian family weddings are big). I landed in Dubai from the US after a 16 hour flight and I had a layover of 1 entire day; the next day I was flying to India from Dubai. My parents and sister lived in Dubai at the time. The next day I was at the airport with my sister for our flight to India and something terrible happened - we missed our flight. It was a busy season and all the flights to

India were full.

I sat at the airport not knowing if we would be able to make a later flight and thought about how a simple little mistake would create a lot of family drama. Would all the people who were supposed to be receiving us at the airport in India, our relatives, be upset? Would we be offending some of them? This felt like it had the potential to blow up.

Missing our flight meant that we would miss out completely on the wedding and not just one or two events leading up to it. It happened because my sister had read the gate number wrong on the boarding pass. At first, I was upset and then I remembered how Zehra had taught me to pre-pave. I remembered pre-paving with Zehra for this wedding before leaving the US, and the first part of my trip from the US to Dubai had gone so well. I wondered... what if I pre-pave again? It would certainly do no harm.

I turned to my sister and said, "let's try this". So, we made a list of our intentions for being able to get on the next flight, and then we made a list of things to appreciate. We offered appreciation her, for me, for the flight, for the airport. We pre-paved our intentions for the upcoming flight and what we wanted to get out of this journey. How we wanted to feel on this journey. I don't know what we did or what the actual mechanics of what we did were, but we definitely shifted our vibration.

In that two hour window we found seats on the next flight which was a huge relief. When I entered the air craft and sat down I couldn't believe my eyes! As I looked over my right shoulder, I saw my most favourite actor from Bollywood, Shahrukh Khan. He sat down in the seat right beside me. He is well known around the world and he is a phenomenal actor; a huge icon in the Indian film industry, and my absolute favourite romantic hero. I couldn't believe it. For the entire flight he was sitting right next to me and he was so polite. The person who was attending to him said we could take pictures if we wanted to. He is the hero I have been obsessed with since my childhood. So, to me it was a dream come true. It just made everything that happened before totally worth it. So that was completely unexpected. We took pictures with him and when we went on Facetime to show everyone, they said, "if this is what comes out of missing your flight you should have just planned to miss your flight in the first place". It was so good.

The Universe has hidden gifts for us everywhere, and if we can align with those gifts and align our vibration with that of those gifts, shift our vibration set-point, then everything falls into place in ways more perfect than we can imagine.

That was a fun story of pre-paving and appreciation and all the wonderful things that practising LOA and maintaining your place on the emotional scale brings to us. I think amongst the other successful manifesting stories this one was a very fun one. And I enjoyed sharing it.

A Note from the Universe
Do you see that it does not take anytime at all for things

to change? Do you see that all you have to do is to appreciate and let go? Do you see how the Universe can surprise and delight you? But perhaps the most important thing to understand is that the Universe does not need your appreciation and gratitude. Appreciation is important so that you may enjoy your physical life experience, for the Universe will never with-hold anything that you desire. When you ask it is always given. When you appreciate, you become one with it vibrationally and then it must manifest.

Little things matter as much as big things

By Nancy Merryl

I'm going to share a handful of little events with you that will show you how I think and how my life works now. Like everyone else, I have had some wonderful things happen, but I didn't know why they were happening and I certainly didn't think I had any role in it. Now, I know better. Over the past two years since I started my conscious journey with the Law of Attraction, I have manifested a new job, a promotion at my new job, and a bonus. I have manifested a huge improvement in my health and lost 100lbs, something I thought was next to impossible. I have manifested many new friends, whereas before I was timid and shy, I have now been voted outgoing and friendly. My life is different now. So here are a few little stories to encourage you to practice a Law of Attraction lifestyle.

It was winter of 1998, I was in Kean University in Union, NJ. It was a very crazy busy time. I had formed my own study groups, did any extra credit, attended tutorials and office hours after class and kept very busy with the piles of homework that I had to do. In addition, I had a part time job and I was in a college level community service organization sponsored by Kiwanis called Circle K International (and yes, I also got an award for perfect attendance). Anyway, I knew I needed a break and just wanted to get away, didn't care where as long as it was some place warm and four days or so. One day I was inspired to cut out pics of magazines as well as print pics of beaches and palm trees. I decorated my tissue box bottom, and sides with these pics (hey I had three roommates, I didn't want anything too noticeable). When I was done, I went for a walk, someone was singing, "come to Jamaica and feel all right" then I turned on the TV, they were advertising Jamaica. So, I wrote Jamaica on the tissue box. I was tired and it was freezing out so as long as the place was warm and had palm trees, I was fine. I put the tissue box in my closet so my roommates wouldn't see it.

My roommates were irritating at times. We all had a lot of exams and once each hour (timed by an alarm, one of my roommates would take a tablespoon and have five tablespoons of coffee and chug water and gargle then swallow, then repeat...lasted anywhere from 20-30 mins). That's when I learnt how to appreciate. I was doing it to take my mind off my roommates' idiosyncrasies. I started saying things like I love how my algebra teacher helped me to study for a test, I love how close the buildings which makes it easy to walk from one class to another. The next night, I closed my eyes and tried to picture myself in Jamaica...how sand felt on my feet, smell of salt water, and the heat from the sun and seeing all those pretty palm trees.

Day three, a friend of mine said, "Hi Nance, did you hear the good news?" I said "what good news?" She said I'll tell you in the evening. That evening she said that Circle K will be going international...the meeting will be in Jamaica. If we go as a group approximately 40 people, we get a large discount. And as easy as that, a month and a half later, I was in a school bus being driven to the airport. Once in Jamaica, several vans were waiting for us to go to the all-inclusive hotel. The convention itself was two days, but I went a day ahead of time and stayed an extra day and a half. I had such a good time, and thought I did this 😊

*****

I made a list when it came time to look for a place to live. At the time I was married, soon to be divorced and needed to leave the two bedroom condo soon. I was actually looking in New Jersey and New York City. I noticed that there was always a short coming in the places I was looking at, for example, one place, had no dishwasher, another place was across from garbage disposal and smelled of garbage, another one had the laundry in the basement and you had to pass several doors that said be aware of dogs...and the dogs growled and woofed at you as you walked past. So, I made a wish list of tiny things such as dishwasher to bigger things like washer/dryer that I wanted and since I hated driving I wanted a pedestrian friendly community, three ways to get into New York City. As I visited with my parents once day I heard news that one of their neighbors' daughter had recently moved to Hoboken. At the time, I had never even heard of Hoboken. I checked it out and it had everything on my list. Washer/dryer stackable, dishwasher, within walking distance to everything and three ways to get into New York City: Path, ferry and Transit Bus.

*****

I was very ill in April 2019, needing me to be in the hospital for six days, and was told that I came very close to dying. I had 31% lung capacity and knew if I was going to continue living, I needed to change my life entirely. I didn't know how though. So, I asked for signs. I started with joining Facebook groups, and affirming yes to better health. I loved the pictures and posts in these groups, but they weren't really helping me and my health wasn't improving. I also felt stuck in life, not much happening and very little changes. Feb 2020, I was looking for something on Amazon and Unlimited 40 Days of Attraction Workbook to Accelerate Manifestations showed up as a recommendation. It sounded good so I ordered it. I lit a white candle, asked for someone to come into my life as a life coach and or mentor. Someone who has lots of patience and that I can learn a lot from. Someone who is an earth angel as well. Then went outside, left an offering of fresh and dried fruit and nuts. Three days later I got the book...I was looking through it and happened to dropped it in a way that it landed on the page about Zehra's Facebook group (on page 3, which is also my confirmation #) The Unlimited-The Law of Attraction Coaching and Support Group. I thought, I wonder if this Facebook group is still active. I took a selfie with the book emailed to Zehra on Feb 09th, 2020 and have been a member since then. When I first met her on Facebook, I knew she was the answer to my asking. Anyways, Zehra became my first ever Law of Attraction; manifestation teachers, who I continue to learn a lot from daily. My health has improved to the point where I regularly run a couple of miles and I have lost 100lbs, and I'm very rarely ill. I have come a long way since learning from her...and the learning continues.

*****

Many little things show up in my life on a regular basis now to show me that I am on the right track. Here are a few examples.

I work from home and at times, sit too long especially when I have a long meeting and can't get up. I looked on amazon for a cushion and didn't like anything I saw. I thought I'd go to the local store my friend Diane owns, Luna Rosa Home, even though I didn't remember seeing any cushions there. I go into Luna Rosa Home and tell Diane what I'm looking for. She starts showing me all these fancy pillows for hundreds of dollars that I didn't think were right. I asked if she had anything in the back and said I don't care what it looks like as I'm sitting on it, not displaying it. She smiled and said wait right here. A few seconds later, she comes back with a cushion and says by law, if an item has an imperfection she can't sell it...she pointed to a tiny dot that if she didn't show me I wouldn't have noticed it and she gave me the cushion for free ☺

I was at work and tired, 3 PM and hot, the AC was not working. I wanted an iced coffee but I already had my lunch break and had no time to get one as I was very busy. I got up from my desk and went to make some copies. I came back to my desk and there was a iced coffee on my desk with a sticky note that read iced coffee with almond milk, enjoy ☺ and I did (it was exactly how I wanted it).

I saw on Amazon a six box set of fall teas, I added it to my shopping cart but never checked out. No time, had to leave for interstate commuting to go to work. That evening, I got a notification to pick up package across the street. A friend of mine had sent me the six box set of fall teas that I just placed in my cart. Same thing happened again, I was low on Chai tea, I was going to get some more sometime soon, but never did. I had it on my list and still forgot to get it. Anyways, I got a notification to pick up package across the street, I was thinking, huh? I didn't order anything. A friend of mine sent me 6 boxes of chai tea.

I was watching the news and as I held a cute owl mug I saw it cracking even as I held it – I knew it was going to explode any second. I ran to the sink just in time as it all fell apart. I said out loud I need a new owl mug. The next day, a friend of mine sent me a cute owl mug from Amazon. Things like this happen for me on a regular everyday basis and I am finally beginning to feel more confident and happy.

I have to say that I have really applied myself to doing the work. Every time, Zehra has given me an exercise to do, I have done it to a T. I participate in the live Q&A sessions on a regular basis. In the beginning I was quiet and didn't ask too many questions, then I started asking, and I found that it really helps to move forward when you ask as question. And now I am in a new place, where I don't have too many questions, but I still show up because I know I need to stay on track and showing up helps me with that. My advice to everyone who is learning to use the Law of Attraction is – be consistent and do the work.

A note from the Universe:
If you want the Law of Attraction to bring you the results you want in life then you must be consistent in

thinking positive thoughts. Your journey is of one, who found a winning formula, got positive results and then instead of using it all the time, you put it away. Finally, the situation with your health forced you to become consistent in doing the work that would move you towards improved alignment.

Things never have to get to such a drastic point if you just take note in the earlier stages and start paying attention to your emotional guidance system.

Remember: *Manifestations are a result of momentum and momentum is a result of consistency.* Consistent negative thoughts create negative momentum that manifests in ways that you do not like while consistent positive thoughts, result in positive momentum, bringing you things that make you happy.

Manifestations are just evidence of how good a job you are doing in thinking your thoughts. When things you want show up in your life, it is an indication that you are doing a good job of thinking, and when things you don't want show up it is time to stop, take note, and do more of what you know is positive thinking – appreciation, gratitude, meditation. When you pay heed, it takes no time at all to change the course of your manifestations. And *the better it gets, the better it gets*.

Manifesting Abundance

By Natalie Flowers

I had basically lived in the same state for almost 45 years. Maybe it was time for a change, but how would I know if this would be a good change and how would I know if it was the right change?

It all started about a year ago when my husband's company decided to expand further into other US states. They had already moved into Virginia and were now breaking ground in North Carolina. One day in July 2020, during the midst of the COVID Pandemic, the powers that be at my husband's company came to him and asked if he would be willing to move from Maryland to North Carolina. He called me as soon as he was out of his meeting and said, "how do you feel about North Carolina?"

Wow, just wow. Talk about change, we would be moving from a place we spent our whole lives, where we were raising our son and where the majority of both of our families were located. This would be a big move and a big decision. Not only would it affect myself, my husband and my son, but it would affect how often we visit with our extended family and who we would see for holiday events. It was almost crazy to think about at first. We had a big decision in front of us. How does this affect our family? What is the work opportunity? What was North Carolina like? Were there good schools for our son? How is the traffic? How are the houses? How are the people? These questions went on and on.

Finally, I remembered my Law of Attraction training and decided to focus on all the good possibilities and/or opportunities that could come out of this move. I started making a list of all the positive aspects I could find about North Carolina and the positives of the job opportunity for my husband.

After a few discussions with my husband and thinking of all the ways this move would be good for our family, we decided we would seriously consider moving to North Carolina.

The first thing we had to do was run it by our son. He was 10 at the time and was heading into 5th grade at a new school. His first reaction was tears, but luckily, they didn't last very long. We were able to shift his perspective and show him some of the positives. We said things like: you're starting in a new school anyway, so if you are making new friends, it doesn't matter if you make new friends in Maryland or North Carolina. We said we would only be five hours away from most of our family, so we could still travel and see them, or they could come visit us. We said we've spent the past five months doing Zoom calls and texting anyway, so we could continue with that to make sure we all stay in touch.

He immediately lighted up and changed his perspective. It was so much fun to see his shift. He started smiling and he even started thinking of his own fun possibilities like: maybe we could get "wired" internet (we had satellite and it was HORRIBLE), maybe he could get a room with a bathroom attached, maybe he could have a room for playing and gaming, maybe we would finally be in a neighborhood with other kids, maybe we would be in a neighborhood where he could ride his bike, maybe he could continue in "live, in-person" school, not virtual, and maybe we could find lots of new things to do and see. He was coming up with a lot of these things on his own, again it was so great to witness his shift. He felt good and we felt good.

We all discussed and decided as a family, North Carolina was an amazing opportunity, not only for my husband, but for our family. We were all happy and excited for this new change and for new opportunities. We said yes to his company and started figuring out how to move and get everything rolling.

To get started, we knew we had to sell our current home. We couldn't buy another home without getting rid of the current one. At the time, the housing market was a little crazy. Homes were selling before they even hit the market in some instances. We knew we had to get right on this.

We called a local real estate agent, who was referred by a friend. He was absolutely amazing. He came to our house, looked around and walked our entire property line. He said he was confident he could sell our home and sell it quickly. He told us to price it at an amount lower than what we wanted to get for our house. Although, that made us slightly uncomfortable, as we needed all the money we could get to help with the move and to purchase a new home, we agreed. He said with a little paint and staging; we would definitely get the asking price and the odds were it would be even more than the asking price. Even though the price was a little low, we took his advice and agreed to list it at his recommendation. We then painted the whole house and staged it, mostly by removing most of the furniture and personal items. The agent then came back when the house was ready, took pictures and prepared us for actually putting our home on the market.

Throughout the entire process, we kept our focus on the positives. We were always joking and talking about how nice it would be to get way more than asking price for our house. We also had heard stories and had some proof of how fast things were selling and how much they were going for in the current market. We were told it was a "seller's market" and all the odds were in our favor. So, we kept talking about how this move would be great and how we would end up with an even better house in North Carolina because the sale of this house. We kept it light, we kept is positive and we kept our faith that everything would work out.

Our house went on the market on October 15 and by October 17, we had 8 contracts submitted to purchase our house. Each and every contract submitted was above asking price. We were so happy and so thrilled that everything was indeed working out for us, it was such an amazing process!

In the end, we accepted a contract and ultimately sold our house for $71,000.00 over asking price, which was way more than we could have ever imagined getting for our house. It was such a great way to kick off our move to North Carolina. We had our proof and big proof this time, that if you stay positive and stay focused on the positive, good things will come our way.

By the way, the sale of that house set us up and allowed us to get the house of our dreams in North Carolina – which is a whole other manifesting story for another time.

https://www.natalie-flowers.com/

A Note from the Universe:
Any decision you make can turn out to produce amazing positive results provided you stay lined up with it by finding things to support your decision. Your decision to move is an excellent example of how to stay lined up once a decision is made.

Many times, people attempt to make a decision by listing out the pros and the cons of the various options they are presented with. This results in split energy – some energy goes towards the pros and some towards the cons. This activates both, and so ensues a sort of pull and push which makes the decision much harder than it has to be.

Remember: *there is no such thing as "the right decision", for all decision have the capacity to make you happy, provided you stay lined up with them.*

Confusion is created by looking for the absolute "right" decision. If you would just ask yourself the question, which feels best, and then follow through with thoughts that support why it feels best, your decisions would be made quickly and easy and would bring you results that would make you happy.

The better it gets, the better it gets

By Nicole Hale

I was so happy when I finally reached my goal weight. After years of dieting and exercising, I had finally lost the pounds I wanted to lose. And not only that, but I had managed to keep them off for good. So, when I decided to have a tummy tuck, I knew it was going to be worth the investment.

As I prepared for my surgery, I couldn't help but feel a sense of excitement. This was a big change for me, but it was one that I had worked hard for and was truly looking forward to. My husband and I had just sold our house and were getting ready to move on with our lives separately. This was an exciting time, but also a little daunting.

As soon as I made the decision to have a tummy tuck, I felt an incredible sense of relief. It was like I had finally given myself permission to do something just for me, and that felt really good.

I knew it would be a big change, but I was excited about it. And my friends and family were all very supportive – which meant a lot to me.

I knew that the surgery would cost quite a bit - around $9,000 - but I was determined to go through with it. It was something I really wanted, and it would make me feel so much better about myself. I paid a $1,000 deposit in January and the balance was due in July when I had the surgery. Because I had the money in the bank ready to pay, I decided to put the balance on my visa, collect the points, and then pay it in full.

Imagine my surprise when I received an invoice from the Surgeon later in July indicating that the balance was paid in full. I checked my July Visa statement and then my August statement, but the amount never showed up. I called the surgeon's office to make sure there wasn't a mistake and they assured me that the bill was paid in full and they were satisfied on their end. The charge never came through on my Visa card.

I kept the $8,000 in my account for a year just in case the charge showed up later, but it never did! This was 4 years ago.

I was so grateful to the universe for this amazing gift that I enjoy every single day. I decided I was meant to have this and so I did.

I had set my intention to have this surgery. I had the money set aside and had no resistance as to how I was going to pay for it. My vibration was high with no resistance. The perfect match for such an amazing manifestation.

A note from the Universe:
Your success with weight loss is an indication of your success in giving up the resistance that you had been accumulating for many years. Coupled with the feeling of freedom from a relationship that wasn't working and you had decided to end, the relief you felt was

considerable. And although you did not ask for this gift of your bill being paid for you, you had been asking for abundance and prosperity for a very long time. The joy of being able to get the surgery you needed returned to you the self-worth that you had packed away a long time ago. The cumulative result of these events was that in a very short space of time you pivoted to an emotional place that was better by leaps and bounds. Law of Attraction simply responded to your improved vibration.

Remember: *self-worth is at the basis of everything you attract*. Your positive vibration brought to you new possibilities that were not available to you before. A big change in thinking happened to you when you finally stopped trying to fix your marriage – you started caring more about your own opinion of you than other people's opinion of you. Remember: *the only opinion that matters is your own, and what other people think of you is none of your business*.

Set the mind free

By Sharon Bachman

"We must do something to help" my son pleaded. He was telling me about his cell mate Bill, who had lost his will to live. My son, Brett, has struggled with addiction most of his adult life and has been in and out of the prison system. He is a very spiritual person. He and I are very close and are on the same page spiritually. He has helped many of the men he has encountered in prison. Being a life coach, I have helped him coach and develop programs to change the way the prisoners think and feel. One of the books I use consistently is The Unlimited 40 Day Law of Attraction workbook.

Twenty-twenty was a rough year for everyone. People needed help more than ever. I wasn't surprised when my son called me and ask if I could help his cell mate.

William (Bill) Rundle is a 76-year-old inmate doing life without parole at Warm Springs Correctional Center in Carson City, Nevada. He has been incarcerated for the last 17 years. He is my son's cell mate. His health was failing and his motivation to live was gone. Then, to make matters worse, the entire prison contracted COVID-19. In Bill's mind, this was his exit strategy, his chance to fade slowly into the sunset. But my son was determined to do everything possible to keep Bill around.

As Brett relayed Bill's story of heart break and tragedy to me, we both cried.

"Come on Bill, get up," Brett pleaded. "You can't just lay there and die, not on my watch. You have become one of my best friends. You're my old Buddy. You have helped me in so many ways, I'm not going to let you die."

In a weak and shaky voice, Bill opened up to Brett about all the heart break and tragedy in his life. As tears rolled down both their faces, Bill said, "I don't have anyone left Brett. No one that cares. I have some family, but they believe I will burn in hell for my sins, and they don't want anything to do with me. I have no joy, no hope, and my health is gone, it's time for me to leave this world."

Brett was determined to help Bill. He explained to Bill how the Universe conspires to help people willing to change their way of thinking. He told Bill to start by counting his blessings as few as they may be. Brett said, "Actually feel gratitude as an emotion. Feel it in your heart and your life will begin to change."

We got Bill on a daily exercise program designed for seniors. Then I sent him The Unlimited workbook, and lessons on gratitude. He began his road to recovery, mentally, physically, and spiritually.

In a letter Bill wrote me he said, "The most important thing I received, were books that helped reshape the way I thought. These books showed me how to put negative thoughts out of my mind and to believe that anything I wanted to receive was possible. If you wish for it and believe it, you can obtain it. The results were simply magical. By thinking positive and following the daily plan, my life has totally changed. I am now motivated and feel better than I have felt in the last 20 years. The Law of Attraction program is amazing. I now have a positive attitude and look ahead to each coming day. If a 76-year-old inmate can find hope and happiness, anyone can. Sharon, her son, and the program gave me my life back".

The letter Bill wrote touched my heart. Knowing I had a small part in making someone's life a little easier also touches my heart. I have endured many of the heart breaks life brings, but I have discovered helping others is the medicine that heals me.

The group of inmates I work with are the most gracious and most appreciative group I have ever worked with. Finding hope and happiness in prison is truly a gift and not an easy task. It proves that happiness and contentment can be achieved anywhere but, happiness and contentment have to start in the mind. Once we achieve true happiness, the Universe conspires to bring us more of the same. Thank you Zehra, for sharing your knowledge and allowing me to pass it on. Together we can change the world, one life at a time.

I have lived the law of attraction all my life. Part of my life not even knowing it. The other half of the time, knowing full well what the power of positive thought and gratitude, could do for me. I am truly blessed in the simple life we have created. My name is Sharon Bachman. My husband and I live on a small ranch, in Northern Nevada, surrounded by beauty, nature, and all our beloved animals. For thirty years, I owned and operated a large, boarding, grooming, training, and rescue kennel. After selling the kennel in 2010, I finished my Bachelor of Arts degree in human development and became a health and wellness coach and owner of Body, Mind, and Soul Support Solutions http://elkolifecoach.com/

A note from the Universe:
Bill's burden had to do with many things. It had to do with his past. It had to do with his feeling helpless because of being incarcerated. It had to do with the additional fear of the pandemic. It had to do with a feeling that his life was wasted. It had to do with limitation and a lack of freedom.

Remember: *True freedom is the freedom of the mind.*

The fact that Bill is incarcerated physically doesn't mean that his mind is incarcerated. Just because the size of his personal world is reduced to the confines of the prison, does not mean the he cannot find a way to be of value within that world.

When Brett introduced Bill to the power of appreciation and helped him to understand the Law of Attraction, he opened a whole new world of possibilities for Bill. Bill stopped focusing on his past and made it his mission to help younger inmates understand the Law of Attraction so that they would have the ability to create better lives upon completing their sentences. He gave himself a means for redemption. For even though the Universe never holds anything against us and is always loving, we often hold ourselves in contempt and look back with regret. Having a new mission in life gave Bill hope and the ability to look forward instead of looking back.

Encouragement from Brett and Sharon went a long way in helping him. Their unconditional love for Bill was the energy that Bill needed. It helped him to feel that he was not alone and that he was cared for. He was not allowing himself self-love and unable to feel love from the Universe, but he was asking for it and so the Universe found a way to respond to his asking through other people.

Often people relate age to physical ability or to the availability of time for the achievement of goals. But age has nothing to do with either. Time is an irrelevant measure. A lot can happen within a very short period of time and people can create new goals and start reaching for them at any stage in their lives. Bill's life has reset. He is literally beginning to live a new life. A life that is much happier. A life that has meaning. A life that is of value. A life in which he still has a lot to accomplish.

A beautiful gift recognized

By Teresa Hulek

I began my Law of Attraction journey in February of 2021. I was a bit perplexed about asking the Universe for a manifestation, to test the concept. I wanted to make sure I asked for something I wasn't attached to that would be VERY clear and obvious to me that it was an answer to my request. I wanted to be confident that the manifestation was in response to my request. I began asking if the universe would show me a HUGE rainbow, so large that I could clearly see every color of the rainbow. I wrote this statement many times over the next couple of months.

On a day late in May, my birthday actually, I took my parents on a road trip across the state. We started out at 4am and headed back in the early afternoon. It began to rain as we drove and my dad was behind the wheel giving me a much needed break from driving. I was watching the rain and scenery as it passed. I glanced down the road through the misty sky and thought I saw a hint of a rainbow but turned my head thinking I was imagining it because I was wishing for it. It was just the rain, I told myself as I turned away. A couple minutes later my dad said, "I can't believe what I am seeing, I have NEVER seen a rainbow that large or that low to the ground, every single color is easy to see. Wow!" I turned back and looked out the front window to see a HUGE rainbow with EVERY color easily identifiable and a couple of small rainbows for added joy. That rainbow was very low to the ground and spread completely across the front windshield. I have never seen anything like it before, and it was beautiful. It's been a month now since we saw that beautiful rainbow but it had enough of an impact that just yesterday my dad commented on what a beautiful rainbow we saw on that road trip we took on my birthday. It still brings me happiness when I look at the picture or think about that wonderful gift I received on that rainy spring day. The Universe sent me the perfect gift, one which I will remember every birthday.

*****

I consider myself fairly new to manifesting but I understand the importance of not creating attachment to the outcome. As a result, I tend to ask the Universe for signs that are linked to nature; on the subject of bunnies and sunrises I find it easy to be lighthearted and without attachment.

I have been working on and thinking about weight loss for many, many years. I have been successful in the past five years, continually learning and working to lose weight and be healthy. I have lost about 160 pounds, but still need to lose more and am working to keep myself moving forward. A couple weeks ago I started walking in the morning during the hour the sun rises because that time of day feels so very comforting to me. As I started walking I began to cross paths with a couple of bunnies. Occasionally, I would see a beautiful sunrise. During this past week I noticed that I am seeing more, and more bunnies. I have seen as many as 13 bunnies on one morning walk and it is very, very unusual for the sunrise to go unnoticed.

This morning I stood on the scale with a tear in my eye. I am nearly five years post-surgical, bariatric surgery, and I am still losing weight. I am still winning this journey. I had lost a pound. As I walked this morning I realized that God/Source, the Universe had taken my love of bunnies and sunrises and helped me to find a new passion and excitement for my journey. My walks started with an occasional bunny or beautiful sunrise. This week I realized that it is very unusual for me to see less than six bunnies while I walk and almost every morning ends with a beautiful sunrise. Every day, I look forward to counting bunnies and watching the sunrise, and this helps me with my weight loss goal. This morning I realized that the fact that the bunnies show up when I'm walking is because the Universe is listening and responding, to both my requests – the request for bunnies and the request for weight loss. How clever to inspire me in a way that I am able to achieve both! It is a precious gift to help me continue on my weight loss journey which is a deep desire that I was not confident enough to manifest. So, the Universe took my simple manifestations and turned them toward helping with something I was afraid to put into words.

We are loved, and we are given more of what we appreciate and it just may be if you look close enough, that it is done in a way to help you toward something that is a deep desire in your heart.

A note from the Universe:
The Universe is always sending signs to help you see how you are thinking your thoughts and where you are heading, but often these signs go unnoticed until with increased momentum of energy they become bigger and

bigger and bigger. You see, the Universe never stops sending signals and each new signal is bigger than the last one, until it finally has your attention.

The Universe responds to every desire whether it is big or small, and tries to fit things together so that you can derive maximum joy from each day – always looking for ways to help you achieve your desires in happy ways. When you start noticing the signs that the Universe is sending you and responding consciously, the creative process becomes more fun. Your awareness begins to improve and you start responding to the cues the Universe send your way in a manner that is deliberate in helping you achieve your goals.

Remember: *desires are not big or small – they are just desires*. It is your perception that adds the size and effort to them.

I know everything is always working-out for me...even when I can't see it.

By Yolanda Correa

I lived this shocking and amazing experience many years ago. Every time I remember it, it gives me goose bumps. It has become my anchor; I remind myself of it every time I forget that things are always working out for me.

This happened in Mexico, I was about 20 years old at the time – I had no idea then, how the Law of Attraction worked. I was at the police station as my boyfriend had been arrested. I was waiting to hear if he was going to be booked. It was late, and I was tired. I wanted to go home since I had to be back really early the following morning for the hearing.

There was a specific policeman who was with me throughout the day. He was attentive and showed his concern about my safety in going home alone late at night. He offered to take me home, and I accepted because truth be told, I was scared about going alone, and I was tired and feeling completely emotionally drained. What could be safer than a policeman driving me home? But the next thing he said actually scared me even more. He said he wanted to spend the night at my house, to make sure I was safe. He said that since I lived alone, he wanted to make sure I wouldn't be afraid, and that he would sleep in the living room. He said his only intention was to take care of me… I felt fearful of saying "yes", something about this didn't seem right. But I said "yes" anyway because I thought he's a police office, he wouldn't hurt me – but something in the pit of my belly felt uncomfortable.

In my heart, I was afraid. I was praying that everything would turn out alright, asking God to protect me. While I was standing outside waiting for him to get his car, a friend and her husband came by just seconds before the policeman returned with his car. I was shocked that she was there with such precise timing since I was not expecting her. I asked her what she doing there so late in the evening? She said that she had heard what had happened and decided to come by to help me.

The only explanation in my mind for her timely appearance was that she was the answer to my prayer for safety. God put it in her heart to help me, which she really did in the biggest way ever. I felt a wave of relief pass through my whole body as I turned to the police officer and said "thank you for your help, but my friends are here now, and I will be going home with them". The voice in my head screamed one word "SAVED!".

To this day I think about the perfect timing and how quickly my prayer was answered, and I feel grateful and appreciative that the Universe came to my rescue.

A Note from the Universe:
This event is indeed evidence that will help you understand the speed with which the Universe responds to your asking when you don't attach any expectations to your prayers. You asked for help without looking for the help to arrive. You didn't ask questions like "is it coming? When will it get here? Who will you send?"

You had no expectations, and that is why the Universe responded so quickly. Your thoughts were not getting in the way and your asking was pure. Remember: *All prayers are answered, and every thought you think is a prayer*. Even when you think you aren't praying, you are thinking and that is the equivalent of praying, because every thought is heard.

An angel rode on the back of my car that day

By Zehra Mahoon

It was a beautiful September day – the sun was shining.
I came out of the grocery store with two bags of grocery.
I put one bag down on the ground, as I reached into my
coat pocket for my car keys – wrong pocket. They must
be on the other side. It seemed easier to put the bag I
was carrying on the back of the car instead of on the
ground. Distracted, and still fumbling for the keys I
reached out to put the bag on the back of the car and
almost dropped it, eggs and all on the ground. As the
enormity of what I saw hit me straight between the eyes
I started shaking all over.

Thank God I found the keys, because I needed to sit
down. Now I had tears streaming down my face, and I
knew I was sobbing uncontrollably – it took a while for
the shock to wear off so that I could start thinking again.

It was early days after my divorce, and my mother's
transition to non-physical. I was almost a year into a
new business, and still relatively new as an immigrant to
Canada. Things were not going well on any front of my
life. As I left the house in the morning I was looking
forward to my appointment that afternoon with a
possible new client. As I turned into the gas station that
morning the prospect called and cancelled – they did not
seem interested in setting up another appointment. I
was miserable. In my mind I had already spent the
commission I would make from this deal.

There was nothing I could do so I proceeded to drive 50 km to work taking the highway – traffic was surprisingly smooth flowing and I could easily drive over the speed limit. All the way there, I thought about what I should do now. I was already working around the clock and with two kids and no support, making ends meet wasn't really possible every month. I was angry with God. Why me? What did I do to deserve this?

I left the office in the afternoon, stopped to visit a client, took the highway going home as usual. Got off the highway and stopped to get my grocery, and then I saw it. On top of the lid of the trunk was my gas cap! I had forgotten to put it back that morning when I filled the that tank that morning.

It was sitting there as if I had just put it there. You don't understand - I drove an old, old car, the gas cap was not attached to the gas tank in any way. I was in the habit of putting it on the back of the car when I filled her up. That morning I was so upset due to the cancellation that I forgot to put it back on. It sat there all day, resting against the spoiler, not nudged in, in any way, as I drove over many pot holes, drove 50 km stretch on the highway at an average of 120km/hr, turned on many streets going to work and then repeated the process again coming home. There was absolutely no way that that tiny little gas cap could have stayed free standing on the back of the car for that long as I drove all day.

All laws of physics were defied as far as I was concerned. I wondered if there really were angels all around us, and if there was one riding on the back of my poor old car that day. I took it as a sign. A sign that told me that nothing was impossible. Miracles could happen, and that all the things I wanted could come about if I just stood firmly in my faith.

I remind myself of this story often, because it is my personal proof that anything is possible. The universe is powerful and the Law of Attraction works to perfection. Do you have a story like this? If you do and would like to share it, I would love to hear from you. Perhaps, we might include it in the next volume of Manifesting Miracles Collection of stories.

A note from the Universe:
The Universe is always guiding you towards the things you want, but when you are worried or anxious or angry, you're not in a place of hearing the guidance that is coming to you. It's like you have a wall around you or a blockage that prevents your guidance to become known. A situation like this happens when the desire is as big as the resistance or negative beliefs on the path to its attainment.

When your desire was magnified and became bigger in that moment of despair, the size of your resistance diminished in comparison to your negative beliefs enabling you finally pay attention to your guidance and see the signs indicating to you clearly that "all things are possible". Remember: *when the desire is bigger than the fears blocking it, then the fears can slow you down but they cannot stop you from attaining it.*

The Boundless School

By Steven Gottlieb

One Spring Sunday, where a lingering May rain made my world in the Ottawa Valley smell like heaven, I received a random text from a woman named Zehra. "I'm an author," she declared proudly. She says she wanted to donate the proceeds of her new book to a charity I manage called the Boundless School.

I was sipping lemon tea in the cozy humidity and couldn't resist a smirk. I typically receive offers like this with a mixture of cynicism - for I have a history of flinching when looking a suspicious gift horse in the mouth. But I am also curious. I google Zehra straight away and learn that she is the real deal as a writer. And a healer and a teacher, so it seems.

I summon my inner Khalil Gibran. Perhaps life is longing for itself on this wet morning. There may be something here.

We chat on the phone. I ask her, "Why Boundless?" "Because nature heals." she says, without skipping a beat.

I've heard this line before. I've used it myself a gazillion times when I hunt and gather charitable resources. There is nothing particularly unique or revealing about this comment. So, I listened a little more. And then we just chit chatted, reflecting on the ills of our times. And that's when Ms. Mahoon revealed her true colours.

I'm still not sure how, but like a laser guided emotional missile, Zehra zeroed in on a pain I carry inside. I remembered thinking she is a master of something. I tried to barricade the pain, but she'd have none of it. With gentleness and sincere caring, her words comforted me. I wasn't expecting that.

Aha! What she's just done with me is exactly what our charity has tried to do with tens of thousands of kids who have trekked to our 600 acre "classroom" 4 hours northeast of Toronto. To learn, to discover and to heal. There is, indeed, some resonance.

And then quicker than the Big Bang fused the atoms of existence, Zehra roped me into writing this blurb you see before you. "Write about your Charity". While I imagine she and I have circled the sun roughly the same number of times, I had just been admonished by a surrogate grandmother to get going.

How to summarize forty years of Boundless?

We are a clumsy utopia. Imagine learning environmental science by creating, tending and harvesting your own organic garden. How about reciting poetry for English class by going on blindfolded night hikes in thunderstorms to find your muse. How about learning math by designing a business plan to manage a successful conservation area. If you plan to create more trails, go out and make them yourselves.

When you come home from a long day, you live, dine and clean side by side with your peers and teachers. And when you lose your shit, you have a caring mental health team to help you find your equilibrium.

All this is set in a stunning paradise alongside the Madawaska River.

Despite these advantages, life can be messy at Boundless. Adolescent identities are being forged. Hissy fits abound. The logistics of running a wilderness therapy school are akin to flying a space mission. And even before Covid, there was a pandemic of Gen Z anxiety and depression.

Boundless kids come from Indigenous backgrounds, the children's mental health system and from Child Welfare Agencies. They have a history of trauma that will make you weep inside and feel helpless to heal. But one square centimetre at a time, kids grow here. And before you know if they are transformed and ready to face an indifferent world.

We try our best. Thanks for standing with us Zehra, and to all of your readers.

Please forward all correspondence to:
Email: office@theboundlessschool.com
Phone: 613-758-2702
Mail: 7513 River Road RR #1, Palmer Rapids, ON, K0J 2E0

About Zehra...

Zehra Mahoon is a master mindset and law of attraction coach and manifesting expert. She is the author of 12 books (and counting) on these subjects and the creator of the best seller: Unlimited 40 Day Law of Attraction Workbook.

After committing to completely transforming her self-worth in 2006, she went from being massively in debt to owning multiple properties and creating a thriving business, as well as healing her relationships.

Zehra's courses and programs helps individuals to identify the blockages that are keeping them from achieving success. She is committed to making it easy for you to understand and apply the law of attraction.

@zmahoon
www.zmahoon.com
zehra@zmahoon.com

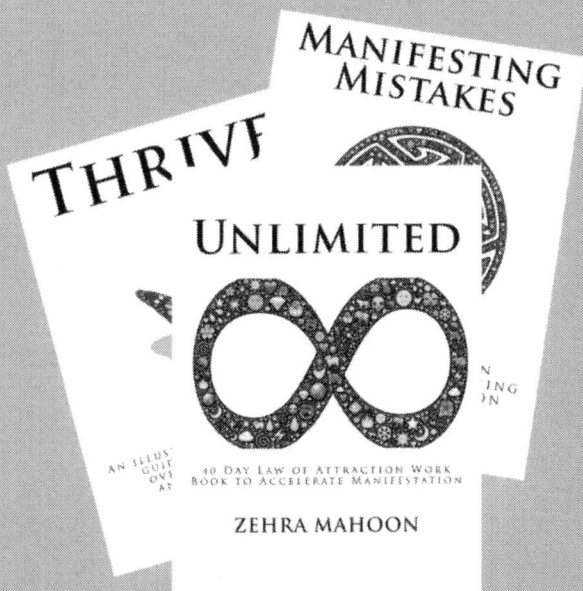

Get all three books in this series

MANIFESTING
SUCCESS SERIES

FIND OUT MORE AT ZMAHOON.COM

Made in the USA
Columbia, SC
09 June 2022